THE
WRITER'S
TAX AND
RECORDKEEPING
HANDBOOK

THE WRITER'S TAX AND RECORDKEEPING HANDBOOK

INCLUDING EVERYTHING YOU CAN LEGALLY DEDUCT

WILLIAM ATKINSON

Contemporary Books, Inc.
Chicago

Library of Congress Cataloging in Publication Data

Atkinson, William.
   The writer's tax and recordkeeping handbook, including
everything you can legally deduct.

   Includes index.
   1. Authors—Taxation—Law and legislation—United
States.   I. Title.
KF6289.8.A96A86   1983   343.7305′2042′0248   83-10110
ISBN 0-8092-5539-1   347.303520420248

Illustrations by Joel Feldman

Published by Contemporary Books, Inc.
180 North Michigan Avenue, Chicago, Illinois 60601
Manufactured in the United States of America
Library of Congress Catalog Card Number: 83-10110
International Standard Book Number: 0-8092-5539-1

Published simultaneously in Canada by Beaverbooks, Ltd.
195 Allstate Parkway, Valleywood Business Park
Markham, Ontario L3R 4T8 Canada

This book is dedicated to my lovely wife, Johna; and to my very special editor, Jody Rein—two people who kept me excited about this project from inception to fruition. It is also dedicated to Krista Marie, my daughter, who was born April 19, 1983. Finally, a special thanks to Mr. Wright, my high school economics teacher, who taught me something much more practical than "supply and demand"—how to fill out my own tax returns.

Contents

Introduction

You've undoubtedly heard Benjamin Franklin's oft-quoted statement: ". . . in this world nothing is certain but death and taxes."

For freelance writers it might be better stated: ". . . in this world nothing is certain but rejection slips and taxes." There are dozens of books on the market to help you deal with rejection slips. This is the only one designed to help you deal with taxes.

Believe it or not, taxes are generally as simple as you want (or allow) them to be. They only get complicated when (1) you want them to be, (2) you become rich enough to afford your own accountant, and/or (3) you're looking for complex ways to shelter income and increase deductions. Don't let taxes scare you. With a little time and effort, you'll find that they are *easy* and, in most cases, *common sense*.

This book will help you if:

- you are a freelance writer who earns approximately $30,000 per year or less;

1

- you simply want to learn to report and pay what you legally owe—and no more.

This book probably won't be a lot of help to you if:

- you are a best-selling author making more than $30,000 a year, have your own accountant, are incorporated, and/or are looking for ways to shelter income, etc.;
- you're looking for ways to evade taxes or "beat" the IRS through illegitimate deductions, "creative" tax shelters, etc.

There are tens of thousands of small-print pages in the *Internal Revenue Code* and *Regulations* to keep you honest. If you have a penchant for miniscule detail, you have months of reading ahead of you. This book, however, is written for simplicity and will cover the basics of all the tax laws that you might encounter while you're in the business of freelance writing. While there are certain areas of taxes that are too complex to address fully in this book, if you're a typical writer (you sell some magazine articles, maybe a book or two, and you don't have so many expenses that you need a full-time bookkeeper), this book should be all you need to do your own taxes.

On the following pages you will find a step-by-step guide to uncomplicating the pertinent tax laws so you can learn to set up your own IRS-approved recordkeeping system and file your own tax returns. It will help you prepare *safe* and *legal* tax records and returns—ones that will provide you with your maximum allowable deductions *and* will survive audits! It may also help you *save* more money in a year than you might otherwise *earn* on any one article sale. "Writing" your own tax return, in other words, can be your biggest moneymaker of the year!

This book should be a handy guide over the years. Appendix I will discuss some of the new rates that will be in effect in the coming years, so you can keep up with the yearly changes in tax laws that might affect you. It also can (and should) be a year-round companion, because much of the information will help you perform the tasks you will need to do throughout the year in order to claim all the deductions you're legally entitled to at the end of the year.

Part I
Writers and Taxes

1

How to Use This Book

During my sophomore year of high school our economics teacher, Mr. Wright, did something I've seen few other teachers do. He taught us something practical. Instead of teaching us only about "guns and butter" and the like (which he knew we'd forget as soon as the tests were over), he taught us how to fill out our tax returns for our summer jobs. When I subsequently informed my parents that I planned to do my own taxes that year, they simply smiled. I *did* fill out my own taxes that year. I was 15. My father checked my entries and math on the five or six lines I was obligated to fill out on the short form. It was correct. Every year since then, my income has grown a little and my returns have become a little more involved; but I've stuck with it.

Most people give me a strange look when I tell them I love taxes. Even when I add that it's not paying the money that excites me, but the challenge of learning all the applicable laws, they still seem to wonder.

Why bother doing your own taxes? Since they are a fact of life, I have found that there is no sense ignoring them (although I suppose one could continue to write in jail!). I also cringe a little at taking them to a professional preparer. First, I like "running my own show," which is one reason I'm a full-time, self-employed writer. While professional preparers are, by and large, very competent and knowledgeable individuals, I don't like to hand over my destiny to someone else unless it's absolutely necessary. Second, communication can break down easily between you and a preparer. Why? If you don't plan to do your own taxes, you're also prone not to keep records. Without records, the preparer has little to go on, and you end up with only a fraction of the deductions to which you're legally entitled. In addition, preparers are liable for interest penalties on any additional tax you may owe because of their oversights. Preparers thus tend to be a bit conservative, giving the IRS, instead of their clients, the benefit of the doubt. This way they lessen their chances of being penalized. Their clients, however, are the ones who ultimately suffer.

If you can take the initiative and courageously prepare a query letter and a magazine article, you can also do the same with your taxes. This book will help you do it, step by step. There is nothing mysterious about taxes. With an open mind and some patience, you should have no problem using this book this year—and in years to come—to help you with your tax returns, ensuring that you give yourself your maximum legal deductions.

The early chapters (2 and 3) introduce the philosophy of federal income taxes and how they apply to you as a freelance writer. The next chapter (4) is probably one of the most important, because it emphasizes the importance of keeping records and receipts. This habit alone can save you thousands of dollars over the years. The more receipts related to your writing expenses that you save, the more you will be able to save on taxes at the end of the year. Won't this place you under the probing eye of the IRS more often? On the contrary. the IRS preys on those who don't keep records. They have little argument with those who keep complete, accurate, and honest records. The IRS says it, and I believe they really mean it: "We only want you to pay your fair share—no more and no less."

Chapter 5 will touch on a couple of real tax-saving programs (Keogh Plans and Individual Retirement Accounts), which, if you decide to become involved, can cut your taxable income each year. The chapter will also help you understand Social Security taxes and your obligations to them as a self-employed person.

Chapter 6 deals with estimated taxes. This is something a lot of writers aren't aware of (or don't seem to pay much attention to). People with "regular jobs" (those who receive paychecks from other people) have their income taxes withheld from each check so that, by the end of the year, their tax obligations are generally met (give or take a small percentage). Self-employed people, however, don't have a boss to deduct their taxes for them. As a result, the IRS insists that you do it yourself so that you're on the same "pay as you go" plan that regularly employed people are. If you fail to pay estimated taxes, the interest penalties you end up having to pay can wipe out any savings you may have gleaned from carefully deducting everything you legally could.

You will probably find yourself referring to Part II of this book most frequently over the year. Listed here, in logical order (and for the most part, by IRS category), are *all* of the goods and services you can legally deduct as a freelance writer. Each section contains not only what you can deduct but how it should be deducted as well. Following the chapter on deductions is the chapter on depreciation. Depreciation is often a little difficult to understand, but since the advent of ACRS depreciation (explained in Chapter 8), it is much simpler than it was in the past. There may be a tendency to ignore depreciation (and the tax benefits it could have for you) because of its seemingly insurmountable complexity. Don't! Particularly if you have a home office, you are legally entitled to sometimes very large deductions because of depreciation. Almost 10% of my writing-related deductions each year come from depreciation.

The final section of the book (Part III) outlines, in step form, how to put it all together; in other words, how to fill out your tax forms, step by step. To make your understanding of this a little easier, I've created a case history in the form of the mythical tax return of Fred E. Lance, freelance writer. Fred is the hapless character you'll see in various cartoons throughout the book. Fred represents a lot of writers—he's courageous, and he's facing the challenge of taxes square on, but he still has that deep-seated fear of the IRS. However, Fred is finally able to accomplish his ultimate task, filling out his tax forms correctly. By the end of this book, I am confident that you will be able to do the same.

To keep you updated over the next few years, I've included future figures in Appendix I. While some other tax laws may change in the future, these are the only changes currently planned. Rest assured, however, that the forms themselves (and their accompanying IRS instructions) will be able to assist you in coping with any future modifications. If you have the heart to delve a little deeper, Appendix II will steer you to detailed IRS booklets on various aspects of taxes you'll be interested in as a freelance writer.

In Appendix III, you will find seven worksheets that I recommend you photocopy and save for your own use. These should be all you need in order to keep accurate records and provide you and the IRS with all the information you'll need to fill out your tax returns properly each year.

Finally, the Index is provided to offer you quick reference to specific topics. When you come across a term or concept in the text that is not fully explained, turn to the Index. In bold print beside the term will be the pages where the topic is discussed and explained in depth. Other references to the topic throughout the text will be cited in regular print in the Index. You can also use the Index when you simply want to look up any questions you have related to your tax situation.

2

Your Tax Status as a Freelance Writer

FREELANCE WRITERS AS TAXPAYERS

Freelance writers are a strange lot as far as the IRS is concerned. We are "professionals without an occupation." Few, if any, of the examples cited in tax manuals for purposes of explaining tax law ever refer to freelance writers. For tax purposes, we are classified as "small businessmen" (referring to the size of our operations, not our physical statures), as "professionals" (putting us in the same league as doctors and lawyers), but more exactly as "independent contractors." Any way the IRS looks at us, though, they often look suspiciously. We aren't necessarily more dishonest than any other group of taxpayers, but as a whole we're a lot less conscientious about taxes and tax records. We rarely keep records and receipts. We don't know how much we earn each year, because we don't receive W-2 forms as regular employees do. We don't have accountants to tell us how much we spent for what and where to find the canceled checks and receipts to prove it. Few of us have any accounting backgrounds, so accounting terms sound like vocabulary for rich people. We're just independent people who want to earn our livings (or parts of our livings) differently from almost everyone else.

Like everyone else, however, we're covered by the Internal Revenue Code (IRC) and must pay taxes. To do so, we have to take a little bit of information from one place, a little more from another place, apply this code to our situation, interpret another regulation for another purpose, and so on. But in the end it all works out. And believe it or not, *it really is easy.*

TAX PHILOSOPHY FOR FREELANCE WRITERS

The theory is simple. You pay taxes on what you earn as a writer. "What you earn," however, is not the total amount you receive for your work, but the amount that remains after you subtract the expenses you incur as a writer. In other words, you must determine what it costs you to earn what you earn.

Example: Let's say you earned $10,000 last year as a freelance writer. If you had no expenses, you would owe approximately $2,300 in taxes (about $1,300 in federal income tax and about $1,000 in social Security tax) on that $10,000. However, in order to *earn* that $10,000, you undoubtedly had to *spend* some money (expenses for paper, postage, phone calls, etc.). Let's say you had to spend $3,000 to earn that $10,000. To determine how much tax you owe, you subtract the $3,000 from the $10,000 and pay tax on the remaining $7,000: approximately $1,400 in taxes (about $700 in federal income tax and about $700 in Social Security tax). In other words, by being able to deduct your $3,000 worth of expenses, you save about $900 in taxes.

What is the income you must report? Simply, income is the money you earn for your writing efforts (payments by magazine editors for articles you sell to them, advances and royalty payments from book editors for books you sell to them, etc.).

What are the expenses that you can legally deduct? This is what Part II of this book is all about. In general, though, to be deductible, an expense must be incurred *directly* in the course of your writing business.

Example: If you drive to and from the library to conduct research for your articles, you *can* deduct the cost of that driving. If you drive to and from the library to borrow a novel to curl up with and read in the evening, you *cannot* deduct the cost of that driving.

Again, ask yourself this question: What does it cost me to earn what I earn? To be deductible, expenses must also be "ordinary and necessary" (as defined by the Internal Revenue Code). *Ordinary* expenses are those that are commonly and normally incurred in your writing business. As a guideline, you might ask yourself, "Would one normally expect that this expense would be encountered by a writer?" For instance, office supplies would be considered ordinary expenses. Medical supplies, which would be considered ordinary expenses for a doctor, would not be considered ordinary expenses for a writer. Necessary expenses don't have to be essential or indispensable, but they do have to be "appropriate and helpful" (Internal Revenue Code language). As a guideline, you might ask yourself, "Would this expense be helpful in my efforts to make a profit as a writer?" For instance, a home office is considered a necessary ("appropriate and helpful") expense, but a stereo system you set up that you claim relaxes you while you write is not a necessary expense. A stereo system would, however, be considered a *necessary* expense for a doctor if he used it to keep his patients relaxed in the waiting room.

ARE YOU REALLY "IN THE BUSINESS OF WRITING?"

Before plowing ahead with any of this, though, you have to prove to yourself and to the IRS that you are actually "in business" as a freelance writer. If the IRS doesn't think you are, the story is quite a bit different.

First question: Is your freelance writing endeavor a hobby or a job? In other words, are you primarily engaged in writing to earn money or to have fun? You can do both, of course, but the key word is *primary*. What is your primary motive?

Whether or not you engage in writing as a full-time or part-time endeavor, if the IRS determines that your motive is primar-

ily profit you will be considered a bona fide small businessman and will be entitled to claim all your legal deductions, even if it means you end up with a net loss at the end of the year.

Example: Let's say you spend $1,000 over the course of a year for goods and services related to trying to sell articles, but you sell only $300 worth of articles. If the IRS declares your writing activity a business, you can claim the $700 *loss* and subtract it from your other earnings, such as wages you earn from being someone else's employee.

If the IRS determines that your motive is primarily pleasure, your writing activity will be considered a hobby. As such, you *cannot* claim losses.

Example: Given the above example, you would be able to claim only $300 of the $1,000 as expenses, and your net income from writing would be $0 (instead of -$700). The rationale here is that, since you would have to pay taxes on the $300 you earned, you are at least entitled to claim expenses against that income, but not losses.

The IRS wants to guard against people who claim losses on "businesses" that are actually hobbies. Let's say a person makes ceramic pieces (ducks, figurines, etc.) at home. She spends $1,000 for the material needed to make and paint the pieces and intends to sell them on consignment at a local store in order to make a profit. However, she is so busy making them, and is also a little worried that people won't like and buy them, that she never gets around to making an honest attempt to sell them (or sells only one or two by chance). She declares that her activity is a "business" and claims the $1,000 she spent for material as a loss on her income tax. Can she do that legally? The Tax Court would probably rule that she could not. Why? Because she did not make serious enough and businesslike attempts to sell her ceramic pieces.

How does the IRS determine whether your writing activity is a business or a hobby? If you were to be called in for an audit dealing with this question, the auditor might ask some of the following questions:

- How much time do you spend writing?
- What do you know about writing as a profession?
- How many rejection slips do you have? (proof that you were making honest efforts to sell your material)
- How much do you earn compared to your expenses? (And are these amounts reasonable?)
- How much do you earn from other sources? (If a lot, your writing might be seen as a hobby; if not, it might be viewed as a business you are engaged in for survival.)

The Code states:

> In the case of an activity engaged in by an individual . . . , if such activity is not engaged in for profit, no deduction attributable to such activity shall be allowed. . . . [IRC Sec. 183 (a)]

As long as you are consistently showing a profit in your writing endeavors, in other words, the IRS will have no doubt that you are in business. It is when you are not showing a profit that they will question your motives.

The 2–5 Rule

If the IRS examines your returns and finds that you have been claiming losses in past years, they may determine that you are engaged in a not-for-profit hobby rather than a for-profit business, in which case they will assess back taxes and penalties for the disallowed losses. If your losses have occurred for more than three consecutive years, you have little recourse other than to try to prove that you are in the writing business for profit. To do this, you must present the IRS with relevant facts related to your profit motive, the answers to the aforementioned questions being part of that information. If the IRS accepts your information, back taxes and penalties may be waived. If they do not, you will be assessed the back taxes and penalties.

If your losses have been limited to three years or less (i.e., you have not had four or more consecutive years of losses since claiming your writing losses), and the IRS wishes to assess back taxes and penalties (claiming that your writing business is actually a hobby), you have another recourse. You may elect to delay their determination until the end of the fifth year. What is this all about? It's called the *2–5 rule,* and it states that you must show a profit in two out of five consecutive years to be declared in business for profit.

> A taxpayer is presumed to be engaged in an activity for profit for the current year if, in 2 or more years out of 5 consecutive tax years, the taxpayer's gross income from the activity exceeded the deductions attributable to it. [IRS Publication 535, *Business Expenses*]

Example: Let's say you began writing in 1978 and realized a loss on your activity each and every year including 1983, when the IRS audited your returns. The number of years involved, then, is six years. You obviously have not made a profit in two out of five consecutive years, so the IRS would assess back taxes and penalties (unless you could prove in some other way, such as providing acceptable answers to the questions in the previous section, that you do have a bona fide profit motive).

Example: Let's say you began writing in 1982 and showed losses in 1982 and 1983. The IRS audited your returns in 1983 and claimed that your writing was not profit-motivated. You could then elect the 2–5 rule, which would allow you to show only one more year of loss in the next three years (i.e., you would have to show a profit in at least two of the next three years). If you did show a profit in those two years, you would have met the requirements of the rule (i.e., you would have shown a profit in two of the five consecutive years 1982–1986). If you did not show a profit in two of those five consecutive years, the IRS would then assess back taxes and penalties for the years in which you showed losses. (Normally, the IRS will go back only three years to assess back taxes and penalties, except in the case of fraud, where there is no statute of limitations. When you elect the 2–5 rule, however, you must also sign a waiver allowing the IRS to assess back taxes and penalties for up to five years.)

If you elect the 2–5 rule and do not meet its requirements (i.e., you don't make a profit in two out of five consecutive years from your writing efforts), you may still try to prove your case to the IRS before it assesses back taxes and penalties by providing convincing information that you are profit-motivated. Again, your answers to the questions in the previous section will play an important part in this determination.

Will you survive the scrutiny of the IRS? If you are indeed engaged in writing with a profit motive and conduct your efforts in a professional and businesslike manner, sooner or later you will begin to sell your work and earn more than you spend. (Aren't I an optimist?) The value of the 2–5 rule to struggling writers is that it offers the opportunity to claim legitimate expenses in the early years (the first three years) without yet making a profit.

3

Sources of Income and Expenses for Freelance Writers

Writing income (what you earn from your writing and writing-related efforts) is relatively simple to identify. Writing expense (what you spend in your writing business—and what you therefore can deduct from your taxes), however, is not quite as simple to determine. Consequently, the second part of this book is devoted entirely to writing expenses. Here, we'll simply look at the tax philosophy behind income and expenses as they might relate to you as a writer. In other words, how does the IRS treat the income you receive and the expenses you claim? To do this, we will look at each type of writing and writing-related endeavor you might engage in and how the IRS treats the resulting income and expenses.

MAGAZINE INCOME AND EXPENSES

If you engage only in selling magazine (or other periodical) articles, taxes will definitely be sweet and simple. With each article you sell, you should receive a voucher with your check. It

17

is simply a matter of saving these vouchers, totaling them at the end of each year, and subtracting your related expenses. This will give you your "net earnings," the amount you will be taxed on as a freelance writer.

BOOK INCOME AND EXPENSES

If you're involved in book writing, there are some other factors to consider (but nothing insurmountable). If your income is a flat fee, it is treated the same way magazine/periodical article income is treated. Generally, though, book income is obtained through either an advance or royalty payments (both, one hopes!). For IRS purposes, advances and royalties are treated the same way, since advances are actually "advances against royalties." (The royalty money doesn't start rolling in until after the advance is repaid through initial royalties.)

There is a form called Schedule E "Supplemental Income Schedule" for rent and royalty income. *Ignore it. Do not report book royalties on Schedule E.* The royalties being referred to here are those earned on certain properties (such as oil and mineral rights, copyrights, and patents *purchased as investments,* etc.). As a self-employed writer, you are the *creator* of the books you write. As such, you are taxed on book royalty income as self-employment income. In other words, if you *create* royalty work, it is *self-employment* (Schedule C) income. If you simply *own* the work (but did *not create* it), it is *supplemental* (Schedule E) income. What is the difference? The biggest difference is that book royalty income reported on Schedule C is also subject to the self-employment (Social Security) tax. This additional tax is required by the IRS.

So far, so good. You report your royalty and advance income from books essentially the same way you report income from magazine article sales. However, there is some debate in the Tax Courts over book income and expenses in general. Here's a brief outline of what's been happening:

Some claimants contend that book expenses (what it costs to write a book) should be depreciated (deducted over the course of several years) instead of deducted (deducted all in one year) and that book income (money earned from advances and royalties) should be treated as long-term capital gain (reported as income over the course of several years) instead of as simple income (reported as income earned in one year).

Other claimants contend that book expenses should simply be deducted and that book income should be considered simple income (both reportable and deductible in one year, with expenses deducted when incurred and income reported when received).

The IRS consistently treats book income (advances and royalties) in the latter way, as simple income, so there is little opportunity to spread your earnings out over the course of several years to level out your taxes. In almost all cases the Tax Courts have also taken the latter stance, allowing writers to deduct their book-writing expenses rather than depreciate them.

Bottom line: if you are not earning many thousands of dollars from book sales and are not incurring many thousands of dollars in expenses from book writing, declare advances and royalties as simple income (reportable in the year you receive it) and claim your expenses as simple deductions (claimable in the year you incur them). If, however, you earn substantial amounts of money and/or incur substantial expenses in your book-writing endeavors, you would be wise to contact an accountant or other tax professional for assistance. Everyone else should report income and claim expenses on Schedule C.

MISCELLANEOUS INCOME

As a freelance writer, you may find yourself giving occasional lectures and/or teaching adult education classes on the art and business of freelance writing. If you are earning money from such activities, it must be reported as income. If the adult education class is conducted through a local university, junior college, etc., you will undoubtedly be on the payroll and will receive checks just as any other employee or faculty member would (with taxes deducted). In such situations, *you do not report this as self-employment income.* The income is considered wages, and, as such, it is to be reported on Form 1040 (long form) where "wages" are reported. Why? You will receive W-2s for this work, and taxes have already been withheld. If you report it as self-employment income, you'll be paying taxes twice.

If, however, you receive *fees* (amounts where taxes have *not* been deducted), such as you probably would for one-time lectures or other related services, you report this as self-employment income, because taxes have not been withheld.

How can you tell if taxes have been deducted or not from your income? Check the stub with your paycheck. If amounts have been deducted from the gross amount for taxes, then obviously taxes already have been withheld. If the check you receive is for the gross amount, and the paycheck stub shows no amounts being deducted for taxes, then taxes have not been withheld.

Bottom line: If the payer pays you for writing-related services, deducts taxes, and provides you with a W-2 at the end of the year, report this income as "wages" on Form 1040. If the payer does not deduct taxes from the fees paid to you, report this income on Schedule C as self-employment income. Nothing but common sense!

PRIZES AND AWARDS

Besides receiving income from your article/book sales and any teaching/lecturing you might do, you may also receive prizes and awards (monetary or otherwise) for your work and efforts as a writer. Are these taxable? Here is the rule:

> . . . gross income includes amounts received as prizes and awards. (b) Exception.—Gross income does not include amounts received as prizes and awards made primarily in recognition of religious, charitable, scientific, educational, artistic, literary, or civic achievement, but only if—(1) the recipient was selected without any action on his part to enter the contest or proceeding; and (2) the recipient is not required to render substantial future services as a condition to receiving the prize or award. [IRC Sec. 74]

In other words, if you engage in any action at all in order to receive the award or prize and/or are required to provide substantial service as a result of the award or prize, you must declare the money and/or item as income.

Example: If you enter and win a writing contest, the money and/or item you receive for winning is taxable income.

If, however, you are the recipient of a prize or award that you took no action for, and you are not required to provide service because of it, the money and/or item is not considered taxable income.

Example: If your town's chamber of commerce awards you $100 as the "village writer" (through no action on your part) because of the publicity you have brought the town by being a successful writer, this $100 is not taxable (i.e., you do not report it as income of any kind). If, however, in accepting the award, you are required to teach a writing class at the local library, for instance, the $100 then becomes taxable income.

This is the key to determining whether prizes and awards are taxable as income: If you're making efforts to earn it and/or provide services through winning it, it's taxable. If you're not (if its presentation holds no obligation, and you expend no effort to obtain it and little or no effort to retain it), it's not taxable.

If you receive a taxable award/prize that is something other than money (an "item"), you must determine its fair market value and report that as income.

Example: If you enter and win a writing contest, and the prize is a pair of season tickets to a local theater, you must determine how much those tickets would cost if you purchased them yourself and report that amount as income.

VANITY PUBLISHING AND SELF-PUBLISHING

Most publishers, of course, pay *you* for the right to publish your book. There are, however, "vanity publishers" where the opposite is the case. You pay them to publish your book and then market it yourself. Are these expenses deductible? If you can show that you genuinely believe you can earn money selling your book and are making obvious efforts to show your profit motive, you should be able to claim your expenses associated with vanity publishers. If on the other hand, you are having your book published by a vanity publisher with little thought of earnings (i.e., your motive is primarily pleasure), or if you say you have a profit motive and the IRS feels otherwise, you will not be able to deduct those expenses legally.

In general, the same is true with self-publishing efforts.

If you are unsure about your status, or if you feel you can claim expenses but aren't sure what associated production costs are deductible and how to report and claim them, contact an accountant or other tax professional.

INCOME INFORMATION

How does the IRS know how much you earn each year? If you are someone else's employee, your employer files a copy of a W-2 form with the IRS and provides you with duplicate copies. As a freelance writer, however, you aren't anyone else's employee, so you don't have an employer to file such a statement with the IRS.

But there are substitutes for the W-2. If you earn more than $600 from any one organization (book publisher, magazine publisher, etc.), that organization is required by law to file, with you and with the IRS, an "information return" that reflects your income for the year from that organization. Generally, they will file a 1099-NEC "Statement for Recipients of Nonemployee Compensation." In some instances, however, it may be a 1099-MISC "Statement for Recipients of Miscellaneous Income." Either way, this is your statement of wages earned from the organization. It helps you report your income accurately and helps the IRS determine whether or not you report your income accurately.

When you receive a copy of an information return (1099-NEC or 1099-MISC), *do not* file it with your tax return. It is your copy. The publisher has filed a copy with the IRS for you.

You still must report *all* writing income you earn, though, whether or not you receive an information return.

Example: If you earn $100 from each of 20 different magazines, you will not receive any information returns from them (because the amounts are all less than the $600 minimum), but you still must report this $2,000 (20 × $100) as income. If you're audited, and you purposely haven't reported the income, you may be found guilty of tax fraud (evasion) and fined or jailed (or both).

4

Recordkeeping: For Ease and Audits

Paul Strassels, ex-IRS agent and author of *All You Need to Know About the IRS* (Random House), in an interview in *Money* (February 1982), said: "Writers are notorious with the tax collector for claiming business expenses for which they have no receipts."

Besides the fact that you are a target for an IRS audit, there are other reasons you will want to keep records and receipts of your expenses.

RECORDS: WHAT TO KEEP, WHY, AND HOW

You must keep records. By law, you must keep records in order to substantiate your income and expenses.

> Every person liable for any tax . . . shall keep such records . . . as the Secretary may from time to time prescribe. Whenever . . . it is necessary, he may require any person . . . [to] keep such records, as the secretary deems sufficient to show wheth-

er or not such person is liable for tax under this title. . . .
[IRC Sec. 6001]

These records must be accurate, honestly reflecting all of your
income and expenses; complete, containing enough information
to substantiate your claims to deductions, etc.; and permanent,
held for at least three years, sometimes longer (see page 36 in this
chapter).

> Everyone in a business must keep records that will help them
> to prepare complete and accurate tax returns and make sure
> that they pay only the tax they owe. . . .
>
> Your permanent books . . . must show not only your gross
> income, but also your deductions and credits. In addition, you
> must keep the other records and data necessary to support the
> entries on your records and tax returns. Paid bills, canceled
> checks, etc., that support entries on your records should be
> filed in a safe place. . . . [IRS Publication 583, *Information
> for Business Taxpayers—Business Taxes, Identification Num-
> bers, Recordkeeping*]

Benefits of Keeping Records

Although the law requires that you keep records of your
income and expenses as a writer, and although it may seem like a
complicated and time-consuming task (which it is not), there are a
number of benefits to keeping records:

1. Each and every acceptable receipt and account of an expense is proof of your claim to a deduction. Without acceptable receipts, an IRS auditor can, and probably will,
   reject your claims, in which case you will have to pay not
   only the additional tax but an interest penalty on that tax as
   well.
2. Records also prove that you are in business for profit. If
   there is any question as to your motives (see Chapter 2), the
   thoroughness of your recordkeeping will stand in your favor
   of claiming that your writing is a business, not a hobby, and

that you can therefore legitimately deduct your expenses.

3. Up-to-date records quickly show your profits or losses. You'll always have an idea of "how you're doing" financially.

4. If you need to file an amended return at a later date, you will often need past years' records to substantiate your claims.

5. Retaining your records and copies of your returns over the years is helpful if you ever decide to take advantage of income averaging. If you don't have copies of your past years' returns, you will have to write to the IRS for a special form to request copies of your returns, fill out the form, submit it, and wait for copies of your returns. It is entirely possible that you may not receive your copies from the IRS in time to file by the April 15 deadline. In this case, if you still wish to income average for that year, you will have to file an amended return. Bottom line: you can avoid the headache by simply retaining and storing all of your own records each year.

6. Laws are often passed that allow retroactive additional tax relief. If your records and receipts don't go back far enough to substantiate your claims to any of this retroactive relief, you will generally not be able to claim it.

7. As you file your quarterly estimated tax payments (see Chapter 6), your current and up-to-date records will allow you to determine whether or not you need to adjust the amount of estimated tax you pay.

8. If you claim depreciation expenses (see Chapter 8), you may be required to keep receipts for the life of the asset(s) to substantiate your annual depreciation amounts.

The Burden of Proof

The primary purpose of keeping accurate, complete, and permanent records is to have substantial proof of your claims in case of an audit. If you show up at an audit with no records, or with incomplete records, you stand the chance of having many of your deductions disallowed.

- *If you have inadequate records or no records:* The IRS will probably estimate your income and/or deductions, reduce or disallow a number of unsubstantiated deductions you might claim, and require you to pay the additional taxes and interest penalties.

- *If you have lost your records but have adequate proof that it was not your fault (e.g., they were destroyed when your house was destroyed by fire):* The IRS may allow you to "reconstruct" your income. However, they will probably use the returns you have filed in previous years to make sure your claims are not out of line. It is, again, to your disadvantage to have lost your records, because you will rarely ever be able to reconstruct all of your deductions.

- *If you have lost your records and you do not have adequate proof that it was not your fault, or you admit that it was your fault (e.g., you mistakenly threw them out while spring cleaning):* The IRS will estimate your income and expenses (usually based on previous years' returns), and, of course, the results will not weigh in your favor, particularly where deductions are concerned. You will probably have many of your deductions reduced or disallowed, and you will be required to pay the additional taxes and interest penalties.

Again, it is always to your benefit to keep accurate, complete, and permanent records of your income and expenses as a writer.

Types of Records

Although you are legally required to keep records, you are not required to keep any specific type of records. You may choose any method you wish, as long as it accurately, completely, and permanently reflects all of your income and expenses.

> The law does not require any special kind of records. You may choose any system that is suited to your business and that will clearly show your income. . . . [IRS Publication 583, *Information for Business Taxpayers—Business Taxes, Identification Numbers, Recordkeeping*]

The law also does *not* require that you have an accountant or other professional keep your records or figure your tax for you. You may keep your own records; in fact, as will be shown in this chapter, you should be able to do an excellent job of keeping your own records with a minimum of problems or hardships. Keeping records is much simpler for freelance writers than it is for most other small business proprietors. Most small businesses (retail stores, service stations, machine shops, etc.) deal with hundreds of thousands of dollars in income each year, have employees whose salaries they pay, maintain expensive inventories, have daily incomes and expenses in the thousands of dollars, etc. Naturally, situations like this generally require the services of an accountant. Even if the small businessman knew everything he needed to know about taxes, he probably wouldn't have the time to keep his own records. As a writer, however, your total annual income may be no more than the weekly gross income of a small retail business; your annual expenses may be no more than the weekly expenses of a small retail business. In other words, it is probably easier to keep records for a freelance writing business than for any other small business.

What Are Records?

Basically, records include (1) receipts (various forms of tangible proof of your income and expenses) and (2) bookkeeping (the method you use to enter and record your income and expenses). The next two sections discuss receipts and bookkeeping in depth.

RECEIPTS: WHAT TO KEEP, WHY, AND HOW

Paychecks

Whenever you receive payment for an article or for any other work you do as a writer, retain the paycheck stub and/or accompanying statement of payment. Be sure this has the name of the publication, the date of the check, the amount paid, and the purpose (e.g., "payment for article"). If the check does not have either a stub or a separate statement of payment, photocopy the check and retain the photocopy. (The cost of the photocopying, by the way, is deductible. See Page 90.)

If you do a lot of work for one particular publication, publication group, or publisher, you may receive, in addition to individual statements, a copy of Form 1099-NEC ("Statement for Recipients of Nonemployee Compensation") at the end of the year. The payer will file a duplicate copy of this statement, which shows the total amount you have earned from that source for that year, with the IRS. *Check the total on this statement to make sure it coincides with the totals of the individual statements you have received throughout the year.* Mistakes can be made. For instance, if your individual receipts indicate that you have received $5,000 from the company for the year, but Form 1099-NEC states that you have received $8,000, one of two things has probably happened. First, there may be $3,000 worth of checks that you haven't received but are entitled to! Second, the company may have made an error in stating the $8,000, but it will be reporting $8,000 to the IRS, even though you only earned $5,000. If you haven't kept track of your individual receipts, *you* may then mistakenly report, and be taxed on, the $8,000. If, however, you report the $5,000 that you know you've earned from the individual statements, and you're audited, the IRS will want to know why you failed to report the additional $3,000. To avoid all of these problems, *immediately* get in touch with the payer and get the matter straightened out. Whatever outcome is finally reached, be sure you have written proof of it for your records.

If you receive advances and royalties on a book (or books) you have written, retain copies of all statements and/or photocopies of the checks, since these are also, of course, treated as income (see Chapter 3).

If you have been paying into a Keogh Plan (see Chapter 5), and you elect to withdraw money from the account, the amount you withdraw is taxable in the year you withdraw it. As a result, you will need to obtain and keep documentation of this income.

Rejection Slips

These are the nemesis of every writer, but they do serve a positive purpose, believe it or not. As discussed in Chapter 2, one of the first tax-related matters you will have to resolve as a freelance writer is proving that you are engaged in writing as a profit-motivated business, not as a hobby. One way to help prove your case to the IRS is to be able to produce the rejection slips you have accumulated. In essence, this shows the IRS that the time and money you have spent as a writer have been for the purpose of sending manuscripts or article ideas to editors for sale and publication. If you have no rejection slips, the IRS may rule that you have not been making honest efforts to make a profit as a writer and therefore must treat your writing as a hobby. In this situation, of course, you will not be able to deduct any of your expenses.

Pay by Check

Whenever possible, pay for the items and services you plan to deduct by check (or credit card/charge card). Although a canceled check (or credit card/charge card receipt) by itself is usually not enough to prove or legitimate a deduction, when coupled with a corresponding valid receipt it will almost always be accepted as proof of your claim to a deduction.

If you are a full-time writer earning and spending thousands of dollars each year, you may, for the sake of convenience, choose to set up a separate checking account for your writing business instead of using your personal/family checking account. This, however, is not legally required. *You do not have to maintain a separate checking account to handle writing expenses.* This decision is up to you. It is absolutely legal to use your personal/family checking account to pay for writing expenses. In fact, most writers do.

When you write a check to pay a deductible writing expense, make a notation of the purpose of the purchase in the bottom left-hand corner of the check. Most checks have a line and/or the word *Memo* there for that purpose. This will help substantiate your claim to the deduction. If you *must* pay by cash, insist on a valid receipt for your purchase.

Valid Receipts

The deductions you claim for retail purchases are often the most difficult to substantiate. A cash register receipt with no other substantiation may not be accepted by the IRS. In recent years the IRS has become more lenient in this area with individual taxpayers who are claiming itemized deductions, but it still expects businesspersons (of which you are one) to have substantially more proof of their claims. In other words, it is to your benefit to insist on a valid receipt.

What is a valid receipt? Many stores, especially office supply stores, routinely provide "counter receipts" (itemized statements that show the name of the store, individual item descriptions, their costs, the total cost, the date purchased, and a notation that you paid for the purchase). These are valid receipts.

If a store does not offer counter receipts, *ask* for them. Often, the customer service desk at the store will provide them if requested. If you cannot obtain a counter receipt, ask the clerk or store manager to itemize your purchases on the back of the cash register receipt and initial it. Circle the total. This may seem like a lot of work, but it can mean the difference between having your deduction allowed and having it disallowed. If you purchase in bulk (buy $100 worth of supplies at once instead of ten $10 purchases, for instance), your tax loss can be substantial if you don't have valid receipts.

If you are purchasing a combination of personal and business items at once, have them rung up separately, write two checks (or two credit card/charge card forms), get two receipts, and be sure the receipt for your writing-related purchase is itemized.

As a rule of thumb, attempt to obtain and retain as much documentation of expenses as you can. A valid receipt for phone expenses, for instance, should be a copy of your itemized phone bill with your business calls circled and notations as to the purposes of the individual calls. Proof of the interest and property taxes you pay each year on your home, which you will need if you claim a home office deduction (see Chapter 7), should come in the form of a statement from your savings and loan association, bank, and/or county assessor's office. A valid receipt for postage expenses is the adding machine tape stamped with the official U.S. Post Office stamp (which any clerk should be authorized to do).

Certain expenses will be impossible to obtain receipts for (photocopying costs, parking meter costs, etc.). For expenses like this, create your own individual receipts for each expense and indicate on them the date, amount, purpose, location, etc. In addition, keep a recorded list of these expenses. (Such a form is provided at the end of this book.)

BOOKKEEPING

Complexity

As stated earlier, recordkeeping for freelance writers need not be complex or difficult. You should not need the services of an accountant, nor do you need an accounting background yourself. Paper, pen, and the ability to add, subtract, multiply, and divide (or use a calculator) are all you should need.

A good rule of thumb to remember is that your bookkeeping should be only as detailed as necessary—no more, no less. For instance, if you have no more than 20 or 30 transactions per year (income checks and expenses), you can list all of them on one sheet for the whole year. If you have numerous daily and weekly transactions, however, you may need a separate sheet for each week, each month, etc. (Recommended forms for computing your income and expenses and for keeping IRS-approved records are included at the end of this book.)

If your only expenses are the basics (paper, postage, etc.), bookkeeping will be extremely simple. You'll be involved with only one type of expense (office supplies). On the other hand, if you travel extensively for your writing, claim a home office deduction, etc., bookkeeping will be more complex, but it should still be within your ability to perform. Here's how.

Calendar versus Fiscal Year

Simply stated, you have the choice of reporting income and expenses either for the standard calendar year (the 12 consecutive months ending December 31), or for a fiscal year (12 consecutive months ending the last day of any month other than December). If you file your personal individual income taxes on a calendar year basis (which you probably do), you *must* also do your bookkeeping and file your business income taxes on a calendar year basis, unless you receive special permission from the IRS. For freelance writers, however, there is rarely ever an advantage in filing on any other basis than a calendar year.

Cash versus Accrual Method

Cash method accounting states that you enter income when you receive it and expenses when you pay them. *Accrual* method accounting states that you enter income when you have the right to receive it and expenses when you incur them or are liable for them. The easiest way to explain the distinction is to cite some examples.

Example: Let's say you submit an article to a magazine in September 1983. You receive a letter from the magazine in November stating that it will purchase the article for $200. It pays on publication, and the article is set for publication in February 1984. You receive your $200 check in February 1984. Under the cash method you would enter the $200 as income in February 1984 (when you received it) and report it as income on your 1984 return. Under the accrual method

WORKSHEET 1: ANNUAL INCOME

Year *1983*

Date	Received From	For	Amount
1/22	Magazine A	Health article	$400.00
2/18	Magazine B	Productivity article	$250.00
4/11	Book publisher C	Book advance	$2,000.00

you would enter the $200 as income in November 1983 (the month you received notice that you were entitled to it) and report it as income on your 1983 return.

Example: You make $125 worth of business phone calls in late December. 1983 and $75 worth in early January 1984. You receive your phone bill for that period in late January and pay the $200 to the phone company in February 1984. Under the cash method you would enter your $200 expense in February 1984 and report it on your 1984 return. Under the accrual method you would enter $125 of the expense in December 1983 (and report it on your 1983 return) and the other $75 in January 1984 (and report it on your 1984 return).

As you can see, the accrual method can be very confusing and time consuming. In addition, if you fail to receive a certain amount of money when it is promised, you often have to file amended returns or make adjustments on your next years' returns. In general, unless you have a specific reason for choosing the accrual method (which you probably would not, as a writer), it makes much more sense and is much easier to use the simple cash method. The accrual method is often used by businesses that stock large amounts of inventory.

Setting Up a Bookkeeping System

While it is legal to set up your own bookkeeping system any way you like, it makes sense and is a lot easier if you set up your expense columns the way the IRS does. For instance, on Schedule C (see Chapter 8), expenses are listed at the bottom of the form in various categories. To avoid having to add to, or subtract from, your own expense columns in order to have your figures fit the IRS categories at the end of the year (a confusing process), set up your categories the same way they do. (The samples and worksheets at the end of this book are designed this way.)

Example: If you claim a home office deduction, you may decide to set up an expense column to cover all home office expenses (interest, utilities, etc.) and enter all of these expenses under that one column. If you also had a telephone expense, you might set up another column for phone expenses. However, at the end of the year, you will have to do some rearranging, because the IRS expense categories are not set up that way. One category is designated for interest and another is intended for combined phone and utility expenses. In this case you will have to subtract your utility expenses from your home office column, transfer it to the utilities and telephone expense column, add it to your phone expense column, and transfer your interest expense from your home office expense column to the IRS's interest column:

Actual Expenses		Your Expense Columns (Not Recommended)		IRS Expense Columns (Recommended)	
Interest	$100	Home Office	$200	Interest	$100
Utilities	$100			Utilities and	
Telephone	$400	Telephone	$400	Telephone	$500
Total:	$600		$600		$600

Every once in a while the IRS will change, rearrange, add, and delete expense categories on Schedule C. Be sure to check each year to determine what the categories are. The forms and samples at the end of this book are based on the categories in effect for the 1982 taxable year.

FILING, STORAGE, AND RETENTION

Why

The statute of limitations for auditing tax returns (except in the case of fraud or where you have inadvertently omitted 25% or more of your income) is generally three years from the date the return was due, or two years from the date the tax was paid, whichever occurs later. In special cases, however, the IRS may wish to go back six years. There is no statute of limitations on fraud. For this reason and for all the benefits cited under "Benefits of Keeping Records" in this chapter, you will want to file, store, and retain your records and copies of your tax returns in a safe place.

WORKSHEET 2: MONTHLY EXPENSES

Month _January_ Year _1983_

Date	Payable To	Check #	Receipt Obtained	Expense Code*	Amount of Chk	Amount Attrib. to Bus.
5	Smith University	1824	✓	5	$118.75	$118.75
9	Fidelity Insurance	1830	✓	6	$220.00	$22.00
14	John Smith – lawyer	1841	✓	8	$50.00	$50.00
21	Jackson Pharmacy	1860	✓	16	$25.21	$8.71
23	——	——		17	—	$2.80
23	Bright's Restaurant	1876	✓	13	$12.44	$12.44
25	Jim's Office Supply	1881	✓	9	$18.75	$18.75
28	Smithburg Post Office	1895	✓	9	$15.00	$15.00

*Expense Codes

1 Advertising
2 Bank Charges
3 Car and Truck Expenses
4 Dues and Publications
5 Education
6 Insurance
7 Interest
8 Legal and Professional Expenses
9 Office Supplies and Postage
10 Rent

11 Repairs
12 Taxes
13 Travel and Entertainment (and Gifts)
14 Utilities and Telephone
15 Wages
16 Photographs
17 Duplication
18 First-Year Expensing
19 Miscellaneous

How

The best way to file and store your records is to staple each receipt to its corresponding canceled check (and include any other information pertinent to that specific transaction). You should then maintain separate envelopes (business size or manila, whichever is appropriate) for each expense category (as defined by the IRS) and identify the envelopes accordingly. As you enter each transaction on your records, file the receipt and canceled check in the appropriate envelope. The envelopes can then be stored in a larger envelope or box at the end of the year with everything else you will be storing and retaining: your worksheets, copies of your tax returns, and anything else that pertains in any way to the IRS. Store everything in a place that is safe from fire, theft, water damage, and inadvertent loss. The best place is a bank safe deposit box.

5

Retirement Plans

THE GOVERNMENT'S PLAN—SOCIAL SECURITY TAXES

As a self-employed person, you are not only required to pay income taxes; you must also pay Social Security (self-employment) taxes (within the limits discussed in the chapter).

> Every individual (other than a nonresident alien individual) having net earnings from self-employment of $400 or more for the taxable year shall make a return with respect to the self-employment tax. . . . [IRC Sec. 6017]

As an employee working for someone else, you would be subject to a Social Security tax, which would be automatically deducted from your wages by your employer, and your employer would then match that amount out of his pocket for your Social Security benefits.

Being self-employed, however, you pay more Social Security

tax than if you were someone else's employee. You pay as your own employer and as your own employee.

Even if you are now receiving Social Security benefits, you must pay Social Security tax on self-employment income.

> You are not exempt from paying self-employment tax even if you are now fully insured under social security or are now receiving benefits. [IRS Publication 533, *Self-Employment Tax*]

In other words, even if you are 70 years old and receive Social Security benefits, if you earn income from your writing, you must still pay Social Security tax on those earnings.

How to Figure Your Social Security Tax

Computations should be done on Schedule SE ("Computation of Social Security Self-Employment Tax"), which must be filed with your Form 1040 and Schedule C.

For all intents and purposes, your net profit from self-employment (final amount on Schedule C) is the amount you are obligated to pay Social Security tax on.

The maximum income that you pay Social Security tax on for 1983 is $35,700. (This amount changes annually, based on the cost of living.) Any additional self-employment income is not subject to self-employment tax.

If you also received wages and/or tips as an employee during the year, Social Security taxes will already have been withheld from those earnings. Since you are liable for Social Security tax only on total earnings (wages *and* self-employment income) up to $35,700 (for 1983), you will be able to subtract earned wages from your self-employment income and figure your Social Security tax on the difference.

> *Example:* Let's say you earned $30,000 from a regular job and $8,000 as a freelance writer in 1983, for a total of $38,000. In 1983 the maximum amount taxable for Social Security purposes was $35,700. Since you already had Social Security taxes withheld from the $30,000 (your employer

took care of this), you are liable for additional Social Security tax on $5,700 ($35,700 – $30,000), *not* $8,000 ($38,000 – $30,000).

Note: Even if the difference is less than $400, you must still pay Social Security tax on the amount, because it is considered income in addition to base wages you received as an employee.

Example: Let's say you earned $35,400 from a regular job and $5,000 as a freelance writer in 1983, for a total of $40,400. You owe additional Social Security tax on $300 ($35,700 – $35,400). Even though this $300 is under the $400 minimum set by the IRS, you must still pay self-employment Social Security tax on it, because the $300 does not represent your total earnings for the year, only a portion in addition to regular base wages as someone else's employee.

Estimated tax payments. If you make quarterly estimated tax payments, you must compute your estimated Social Security tax in addition to your estimated income tax. Make your estimated tax payments based on the total of the two taxes (see Chapter 6).

No deduction for Social Security tax payments. Because the Social Security tax is a form of income tax, you may *not* deduct the payments you make as either a business expense (Schedule C) or a personal deduction (Schedule A) (see Chapter 7).

For future years' Social Security Self-Employment tax percentages, see Appendix I.

YOUR PLAN—KEOGHS AND IRAs

Guidelines for Individual Retirement Accounts (IRAs) and retirement accounts for the self-employed (Keoghs) are complex. The Internal Revenue Code covers retirement and pension plans in 92 small-print, single-spaced pages. A plethora of magazine articles and numerous books have been written on the subject of IRAs and Keoghs. This part of Chapter 5 unit will outline the programs in general. For specific details that would apply to the particular plan you might be interested in, the most expeditious avenue is to do some additional reading on the subject (in books and magazine articles) *and* discuss the matter with an agent of an organization that offers such plans (banks, insurance companies, savings and loan associations, etc.). This research should tell you: (1) what the plans are, (2) their general requirements, (3) their potential benefits and drawbacks, (4) who offers them and how to set them up, and (5) how to make contributions and withdrawals.

Keoghs

As a self-employed person you probably don't enjoy the benefits of a company retirement program (unless you are also employed elsewhere in addition to being a freelance writer).

Realizing that self-employed people might have a hard time living on Social Security benefits alone for retirement purposes, Congress passed the Self-Employed Individual's Retirement Act in 1962. Since that time it has been updated and liberalized extensively. Changes now occur almost annually.

Essentially, the plan (called a Keogh Plan) allows self-employed individuals to place a certain amount of their annual income into a retirement account, the proceeds of which can be drawn out upon retirement (or disability).

The money you place into a Keogh is deductible. In other words, if your annual income is $10,000 and you deposit $1,000 of that into a Keogh account, you are taxed only on $9,000 of income for the year, *not* on $10,000. While your deposits accumulate over the years, interest also accumulates. When you retire (or are permanently disabled), you can begin to draw out the money and interest to supplement your Social Security benefits. When you retire, however, you will be taxed on the money you draw out of your Keogh account. The assumption is, though, that by your retirement years you will be earning substantially less than you currently earn, so your withdrawals will be taxed at a lower rate than your deposits would be now.

You can begin withdrawing from your Keogh account at age 59½ (or at any age, if you become permanently disabled and are unable to work). You *must* begin withdrawing it by age 70½.

In the 1983 tax year (taxes you will be paying by April 1984) you may contribute a maximum of 15% of your earned income or a maximum of $15,000, whichever is *less*.

IRAs

Individual Retirement Accounts (IRAs) are the employed person's counterpart of Keogh Plans. However, beginning in 1982, they were liberalized to allow self-employed persons to invest in them as well. As a result, you may now contribute to both a Keogh and an IRA.

The tax advantages for IRAs are similar to those for Keoghs. For instance, if you earn $10,000 and deposit $1,000 of that into an IRA, you are taxed only on $9,000 of income for the year, not on $10,000.

As with Keoghs, the intricacies of IRAs are complex. In general, though, you need to be aware of two main points:

1. You may contribute up to $2,000 of your income in 1983 to an IRA.
2. Generally, restrictions on IRAs are similar to those on Keoghs (penalties for early withdrawal, ages when you may and must begin withdrawing from the account, and types of approved plans).

Again, consult with appropriate individuals for details.

6

Estimated Taxes

IRS policy (as directed by Congress) is to collect taxes on a "pay as you go" basis. The best example of this is the standard paycheck of a regularly employed person. A certain amount is deducted from each check by the employer for taxes (federal and state) and Social Security. In this way most people have paid most of their taxes (or all of their taxes, or maybe even more taxes than necessary) by the end of the year. As a result, they have to pay a small additional amount, they pay nothing, or they are owed a refund.

As a writer, however, you do not have taxes withheld on the checks you receive for your work. As a result, by the end of the year you will have paid no taxes to the IRS on your writing income. Can you simply pay it all in one lump sum when you file your return? If the amount is very small, you can. The larger the amount gets, however, the greater the problem becomes, because the IRS requires that you must have paid at least 80% of your total tax due by the time you file your annual tax return. If you have not paid this 80% or more, you will be subject to a stiff interest penalty, which fluctuates with the current prime interest rate at that time.

Example: Let's say you earned $5,000 from a regular job and $5,000 from writing. The appropriate amount of taxes (about $400) was withheld from your regular income, but none was withheld from your writing income. With $10,000 of income, your tax bill would be about $1,700 (about $1,200 in income tax and about $500 for Social Security taxes). Since 80% of $1,700 is $1,360, the $400 you have already paid is $960 short of the minimum amount you are required to have paid. You would therefore be assessed interest on the $960 you still owe. (This is a hypothetical example in terms of the tax amounts due, because other factors, such as exemptions, would come into play on your tax return. The example is intended only to illustrate how your writing income, with no taxes withheld, can mean you will owe an interest penalty when you file your tax return.)

In order to avoid the interest penalty for not having paid enough taxes by the end of the year, you should make tax payments to the IRS on a quarterly (four times per year) basis. To do this, obtain a copy of Form 1040-ES ("Declaration of Estimated Tax for Individuals"). This form contains a worksheet you can use to estimate how much money you will earn during the year, how much will be deducted in taxes (from other sources of income), and how much you will still owe in taxes (because of your writing or other self-employment income). When you have completed the worksheet, you will end up with the total estimated taxes you should pay for the year. Divide that amount by four and pay the first quarterly installment with your tax return for the previous year (i.e., file your first quarterly payment for the 1984 tax year with your 1983 tax year return, which you must file by April 15, 1984). Do not include the worksheet with your return. It is yours to keep. File only the Form 1040-ES quarterly payment voucher.

You may find in completing the worksheet that you will owe no estimated taxes. This might occur, for instance, if you have substantial sources of income where taxes are deducted with each check and you have only a small amount of writing income. If you find that you will not have to pay estimated taxes, you can disregard the form. To help you determine whether or not you need to file estimated taxes, use the chart on the following page.

There are five reasons accepted by the IRS for not paying estimated taxes even though you have not paid the required 80% by the end of the year. These are, however, very specific and very complex and in most cases would not apply to the average writer. If you wish to look into them, though, you can obtain IRS Publication 505, *Tax Withholding and Estimated Tax.*

Estimated taxes should be paid in four equal quarterly installments. File the first installment with your tax return for the previous year (i.e., if you are filing your 1983 tax return on April 15, 1984, you should include the first installment of your estimated tax liability, along with the 1040-ES Declaration Voucher, for the 1984 tax year). When the IRS receives your first installment payment and Declaration Voucher it will forward you vouchers to include with your next three installment payments. They are generally due on these dates each year:

> Payment 1: April 15 (with previous year's tax return)
> Payment 2: June 15
> Payment 3: September 15
> Payment 4: January 15 (of the following year)

If the 15th falls on a weekend or holiday, the payment is due on the next business day.

The IRS will not notify you when your estimated payments are due. It is up to you to remember when they are due and to file them by the appropriate dates.

If, over the course of the year, you see that your writing income will be significantly more or less than you originally estimated, you may need to make the necessary adjustments, file an amended declaration, and file the new estimated tax due in equal amounts over the remaining periods.

Example: Let's say you find that your tax liability will be about $3,000 for the year, yet only $2,000 of it is being

Start here

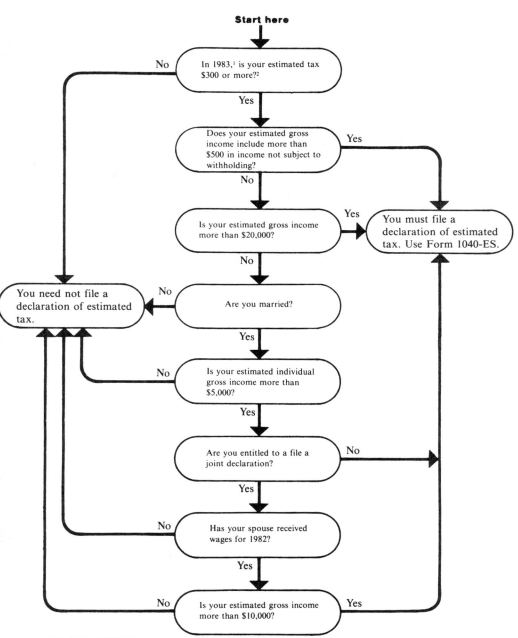

In 1983,[1] is your estimated tax $300 or more?[2]

No → You need not file a declaration of estimated tax.

Yes ↓

Does your estimated gross income include more than $500 in income not subject to withholding?

Yes → You must file a declaration of estimated tax. Use Form 1040-ES.

No ↓

Is your estimated gross income more than $20,000?

Yes → You must file a declaration of estimated tax. Use Form 1040-ES.

No ↓

Are you married?

No → You need not file a declaration of estimated tax.

Yes ↓

Is your estimated individual gross income more than $5,000?

No → You need not file a declaration of estimated tax.

Yes ↓

Are you entitled to a file a joint declaration?

No → You must file a declaration of estimated tax. Use Form 1040-ES.

Yes ↓

Has your spouse received wages for 1982?

No → You need not file a declaration of estimated tax.

Yes ↓

Is your estimated gross income more than $10,000?

No → You need not file a declaration of estimated tax.

Yes → You must file a declaration of estimated tax. Use Form 1040-ES.

[1]For 1984 and 1985 figures, see Appendix I.

[2]Estimated tax is the total of your expected income tax and self-employment tax minus your expected withholding and credits. Do not include minimum tax or alternative minimum tax.

withheld from other wages. You will owe, in other words, an additional $1,000 in taxes. Pay this $1,000 over the course of the year in four equal installments of $250 each. Let's say that you pay the first $250 on April 15 and the second $250 on June 15. Then your writing becomes really profitable in July and you estimate you'll owe, instead of $1,000 in additional taxes, $1,400 in additional taxes. You've already paid a total of $500 in your first two installments (April and June). When you file your amended declaration, you'll be required to pay another $900 over the two remaining periods ending in September and January ($1,400 owed minus $500 already paid equals $900 still owed). You would pay that additional $900 in two equal installments when you file your final two declarations and payments. Thus, your third installment (payable September 15) would be $450; your fourth installment (payable January 15 of the next year) would also be $450:

Payment 1, April 15: $250⎤ ⎡when you estimated owing $1,000
Payment 2, June 15: $250⎦ ⎣in additional taxes

Payment 3, Sept. 15: $450⎤ ⎡when you realized you'd actually
Payment 4, Jan. 15: $450⎦ ⎣owe $1,400 in additional taxes
              $1,400

Note: If you estimated during the year that you would end up owing *less* tax than you originally estimated, you would also file an amended return, estimating the final installments *downward,* instead of upward:

Payment 1, April 15: $250⎤ ⎡when you estimated owing $1,000
Payment 2, June 15: $250⎦ ⎣in additional taxes

Payment 3, Sept. 15: $100⎤ ⎡if you realize you'll only owe
Payment 4, Jan. 15: $100⎦ ⎣$700 in additional taxes
              $700

If your estimates are still off by the time you file your annual tax return, and you have not paid at least 80% of your tax, you should fill out Form 2210 ("Underpayment of Estimated Tax by Individuals") and file it with your annual tax return. On this form you can compute the interest penalty you will owe and add this amount to the additional tax you owe.

If you find that you have *overpaid* your estimated tax for the previous year, you can have it credited to this year's estimated tax payments, or you may apply for a refund.

You cannot deduct any interest penalty you pay on underestimated tax (i.e., you can't claim the penalty as an interest deduction on either Schedule A or Schedule C).

This has been a brief and simple discussion of estimated taxes. If you find your situation more complex than explained above, or if you wish further information on the topic, you should consult an accountant or another tax professional.

Part II

Expenses

This is where things begin to get fun. Expenses are the area of taxes I personally find the most challenging and therefore the most enjoyable. The IRS is very open about the fact that it does not want anyone to have to pay more than his or her fair share of taxes, and I agree totally. Unfortunately, all too many people, particularly writers (who are not known for their interest in math and accounting), fail to claim all the expenses they are legally entitled to. Furthermore, tax professionals, while they are well versed in almost all aspects of tax law, can still miss some of your expenses, particularly if you are not able to communicate all of them to the preparer. If at all possible, you should familiarize yourself intimately with all of the following writing-related expenses so that you are aware of everything you can legally deduct.

Below you will find brief definitions of the types of expenses you might incur and examples of each. Following that, chapters 8 and 9 will help you claim the specific maximum expenses allowed by law.

Simply stated, expenses are the costs you incur related to your writing business (the money you must spend in order to earn money from freelance writing).

For freelancers, expenses can be claimed in three different ways: *deductions, depreciation,* and *investment credits.*

DEDUCTIONS

Deductions are expenses you can claim in the year you incur the expenses. Most expenses you will incur as a freelance writer will probably fall into the deduction category (office supplies, travel and entertainment, utilities and telephone expenses, etc.).

Example: If you earned $1,000 as a freelance writer and had no expenses, you would pay tax on $1,000. If, however, you spent $100 during that year for office supplies, etc., you could claim that $100 expense as a deduction, subtract it from your $1,000 income, and pay taxes on only $900.

DEPRECIATION

You may incur some expenses that the IRS requires you to deduct over a period of several years (home office, office equipment, etc.): in general, property that has a useful life of more than one year. This is called *depreciation.* The IRS's rationale is that if you are using something for more than one year, you should not be able to deduct all of the expense in the first year. For instance, if you spend $10,000 for office equipment, you may not deduct that $10,000 in the year in which you purchase the equipment. The equipment will last for a few years, so the IRS requires that you depreciate the equipment over its useful life. You would, in other words, deduct some of the $10,000 the first year, some more of it the second year, etc., until the last year, when you would deduct the final remaining amount. As a result, you would be deducting the $10,000 over a number of years (a little bit at a time) instead of deducting it all the first year. (For a detailed explanation of depreciation, see Chapter 8.)

INVESTMENT CREDIT

As a way of stimulating the economy, Congress offers businesses a tax incentive to purchase equipment (depreciable property). This incentive is called an *investment credit*. An investment credit means that you can deduct a certain percentage of the price you paid for your depreciable property from the tax you owe instead of from your income. Let's say you earned $5,000 and owed tax of $400 on that. If you could claim an investment credit of $100, you would be able to subtract the $100 from the $400 you owed in taxes (thus owing only $300 in taxes). You would *not* deduct the $100 from the $5,000 and have a taxable income of $4,900. (Tax on $4,900 might be $385. If the $100 credit were only a deduction, in other words, you'd only save about $15. As a credit, you actually save the full $100.)

Chapter 7 explains the various deductions you might incur in your writing business. Following that (in Chapter 8) are in-depth discussions of depreciation and investment credits.

7

Deductions

In this chapter you will find a number of topics that can run anywhere in length from a couple of paragraphs to a few pages. Is there any rhyme or reason to the way these categories are set up? Yes. These are the categories the IRS uses on the tax form (Schedule C) that you will be filling out. Learning about deductions this way, in other words, will prepare you best for understanding and filling in your tax form.

ADVERTISING

Although it is unlikely that you will advertise much in your career as a writer, any advertising costs that are associated with your writing are deductible, provided they are reasonable and bear a reasonable relationship to your writing.

These are some examples of deductible advertising:

- If you are teaching a writing course or giving a lecture related to writing or your work, any ads for this are deductible.

- If you self-publish your book, you can deduct the cost of advertising it. The IRS often decides whether or not self-publishing or vanity publishing costs are deductible based on the intent of the author: Is the individual trying to make a profit on the book? If it seems evident that you are trying to make a profit, your expenses in connection with the book will probably be allowed as deductions. If you don't seem to have a profit motive, your expenses will probably be disallowed as deductions. Advertising is one thing you would have in your favor in terms of trying to prove you have a profit motive. If you are purchasing ads to sell your book, in other words, it shows that you are interested in selling the book and trying to make a profit on it.

Advertising to support or defeat a political candidate, cause, or piece of legislation is not deductible. If, for instance, a politician introduced a bill that you feel would adversely affect writers, you would not be able to deduct the cost of any ads you placed to sway public opinion against the politician and/or legislation.

Advertising costs are generally deductible during the year in which you paid for them, provided you are using the cash method of accounting (see Chapter 4). For instance, if you take out a one-year ad in your local newspaper to sell your book from June 1983 through June 1984 and pay for the whole year in June 1983, the whole cost of advertising is deductible in the 1983 tax year.

BANK CHARGES

If you maintain a separate checking account for your writing business, you may deduct bank charges in relation to that account (cost of checks, monthly service charges, etc.).

If you use your personal/family checking account for both personal/family needs and your writing needs, you may deduct the appropriate portion of charges related to your writing. For instance, if one out of every five checks you write is related to your writing business, you can deduct one-fifth of the cost of your checks, one-fifth of the monthly service charge, etc.

CAR AND TRUCK EXPENSES

Driving your car can drive down the amount of taxes you have to pay. How? Any driving you do related to your writing business is deductible. If you drive to and from an interview you're conducting for an article or a book you're writing, the expenses involved with the driving are deductible. If you drive to the office supply store to purchase supplies for your writing, the expenses are deductible. If you drive to the library to do research for something you're writing, the expenses are deductible.

Ways to Claim Expenses

If you do not own your vehicle, you may deduct the expenses for either the rent or the leasing charges you pay on the vehicle. If you rent or lease the vehicle, simply report the expenses on Schedule C under either "Car and Truck Expenses" or "Rent on Business Property." If, however, you rent or lease a vehicle while away from home on a business trip, claim your expenses under "Travel and Entertainment" on Schedule C.

If you own your own vehicle, you may deduct expenses in one of two ways: the standard mileage allowance (the figures for which are set by the IRS), or the actual operating costs (the individual expenses connected with the vehicle).

Regardless of which way you claim expenses on a vehicle— rent/leasing, standard mileage allowance, or actual operating costs—you may deduct expenses only for the business use (not the personal use) of the vehicle. For instance, if you use your vehicle 40% for your writing business and 60% for personal use, you may deduct only 40% of your vehicle expenses.

Standard Mileage Allowance

This is the simplest way to claim auto/truck expenses, but it may or may not be the most financially advantageous for you. If your car is not fully depreciated, you may deduct 20¢ per mile (in 1982) for the first 15,000 business miles you drive per year. You may deduct 11¢ per mile for any business miles in excess of 15,000 business miles per year.

Example: If your car is not fully depreciated and you drive 18,000 business miles in 1982, you may deduct $3,300:

$$
\begin{array}{r}
20\text{¢} \times 15,000 \text{ miles} = \$3,000 \\
\underline{11\text{¢} \times 3,000 \text{ miles} = \$330} \\
18,000 \text{ miles} = \$3,300
\end{array}
$$

Example: If your car is fully depreciated and you drive 18,000 business miles in 1982, you may deduct $1,980 (11¢ × 18,000 miles = $1,980).

How do you determine if your car is fully depreciated? If you use the standard mileage allowance each and every year you own the vehicle to figure your vehicle expenses, your vehicle is considered fully depreciated for IRS purposes either (1) after five years of business use or (2) after 60,000 miles of business use at the maximum rate, whichever comes first.

Example: If you have been using your vehicle for only four years for writing purposes, you may deduct 20¢ per mile for the first 15,000 miles you drive in a year and 11¢ per mile for the excess of that 15,000 miles (in 1982). If you have been using your vehicle for six years for writing purposes, you may deduct only 11¢ per mile for all business miles driven in the sixth year and following years.

If, however, you elected to deduct actual operating costs for one or more years during the time you used your vehicle for writing purposes, your car is considered fully depreciated at the end of the period you estimated to be its useful life, generally three years (see Chapter 8).

Example: If you deducted actual operating costs for one or more of the first three years you used your vehicle for writing purposes and claimed a useful life of three years on the vehicle for depreciation purposes, you may claim only 11¢ per mile during the fourth year of business operation of the vehicle if you choose the standard mileage allowance for that fourth year. (Again, the 11¢ is the rate for 1982.)

Note: If you use the standard mileage allowance, you may also deduct any parking fees and road/bridge tolls you incur and interest and state/local taxes paid on the purchase of the vehicle. You may also be able to claim an investment credit (see Chapter 8). No other expenses may be deducted if you use the standard mileage allowance.

Actual Operating Costs

If you choose not to take the standard mileage allowance, you may deduct all of your business-related expenses in operating your vehicle. These include:

gasoline

oil

repairs

washing/waxing

garage rent

insurance

license plates

driver's license

parking costs

bridge/road tolls

interest on the purchase price
  of the vehicle

state/local taxes

city/local stickers

auto club membership

lubrications

towing costs

antifreeze/fluids

title registration fees

all other supplies/services with
  useful life of less than a year

depreciation*

Records

In all cases, you should keep the following records related to the business use of your vehicle:

- the year you placed the vehicle in business (writing) use
- the total number of miles driven in a year (business and personal combined)
- the total number of business miles driven in a year

If you choose to deduct actual operating costs, you must also keep records of gasoline purchases, repair bills, etc.

---

*on the vehicle itself and items with a useful life of a year or more, such as batteries, tires, etc.

Which Method Is Better for You?

It depends. If you don't want to bother keeping track of the records required for deducting actual operating costs, you may simply wish to claim the standard mileage allowance. If you do wish to deduct actual operating costs, but you lose your records, you will probably have to take the standard mileage allowance. If you want to choose the most economical method, you should figure your expenses both ways each year and choose the method that shows the greater expense.

You can change back and forth each year (from standard mileage allowance to actual operating costs to standard mileage allowance, etc.) unless you claim ACRS depreciation (see Chapter 8) on your car, in which case you may not use the standard mileage allowance again in claiming expenses for that particular vehicle. (You may, of course, begin using the standard mileage allowance again when you purchase a different vehicle.)

WORKSHEET 3: STANDARD MILEAGE ALLOWANCE

Date	Description	Purpose	Mileage			(x) Rate	(=) Amount
			Start	End	Total		
2/14/82	Smithtown - Jonestown (+ back)	Jack Thomas interview	28,214	28,280	66	20¢	$13.20
4/11/82	Smithtown - Troy (+ back)	Writer's Club meeting	29,522	29,607	85	20¢	$17.00
5/5/82	Smithtown - Jonestown - Troy - Jonestown - Smithtown	Research for investing article	31,002	31,208	206	20¢	$41.20

WORKSHEET 4: ACTUAL OPERATING COSTS
(Itemized Auto Expenses)

Mileage at end of year	_34,218_
Mileage at beginning of year	− _25,562_
Total miles driven during year	_8,656_
Total business miles driven during year	_2,885_
Percent of vehicle use for business (total business miles ÷ total miles)	_33⅓_%

Individual expenses

auto club membership	$ _20.00_
bridge/road tolls	$ _5.85_
depreciation of vehicle	$_418.00_
depreciation on misc. items	$ _26.18_
fluids/lubricants/etc.	$ _41.00_
garage rent	$ _—_
gasoline	$ _918.00_
insurance	$ _120.00_
interest	$ _—_
licenses/plates/stickers/etc.	$ _45.00_
misc. deductible items	$ _—_
parking costs	$ _18.75_
repairs	$ _421.00_
state and local taxes	$ _—_
towing	$ _—_
washing and waxing	+ $ _12.00_
Total individual expenses	$ _2045.78_
Percentage of business use (from above)	_33⅓_%
Total deductible	$ _681.93_

WORKSHEET 5: COMPARISON OF ITEMIZED AUTO EXPENSES VERSUS STANDARD MILEAGE ALLOWANCE

Standard Mileage Allowance

Total amount (from business miles driven) (Total of Worksheet 3)	$ _577.00_
Interest (on purchase of vehicle)	$ ——
State/local taxes (on purchase of vehicle)	$ ——
Parking fees and bridge/road tolls	+ $ _24.60_
Total amount deductible	$ _601.60_

Itemized Auto Expenses (Actual Operating Costs)

Total from Worksheet 4 $ _681.93_

Which is larger?

☐ Standard Mileage Allowance

☒ Actual Operating Costs

Choose this method for the year.*

---

* See Chapter 7 for limitations on choice based on use of depreciation.

DUES AND PUBLICATIONS

For most professionals and other businessmen, dues and publications fit together well. They are often one and the same. Why? They generally refer to the expenses professionals and businessmen have in relation to professional societies, organizations, and associations they belong to (annual membership dues) and to the trade and technical publications that these organizations publish (subscription costs).

For writers this may also be the case. For example, you may belong to a writer's organization that publishes a magazine, and you pay dues to the organization and subscribe to its magazine. However, writers have the opportunity to deduct many more of the publications that they pay for. Here are the dues you can deduct and the publications you might use and how to deduct them.

Dues

Like professionals and businessmen, you can deduct the cost of memberships to professional writing societies, associations, organizations, etc.

Publications

You can deduct the writing-related costs of every magazine you purchase. These generally fall into three categories:

- magazines that will help you as a writer, such as *Writer's Digest, The Writer,* etc.
- magazines that publish articles or other information that you need for research you are doing for an article or book that you're writing
- magazines that you think you might like to write for (you would want to purchase the magazines in order to determine whether or not they are ones you could, or would want to, write for)

Your methods of purchase would also fall into three categories:

- subscriptions to the magazines
- individual newsstand purchases of the magazines
- direct individual purchases of the magazines from the publishers, which you might have to do if you aren't able to locate them on your newsstand and/or if you don't want to subscribe to them

Be sure you can substantiate to the IRS that your magazine purchases are indeed related to your writing. For instance, if you deduct your subscription costs to *Buzz Magazine,* because you are interested in writing for the magazine, be sure you have some copies of correspondence from *Buzz Magazine* (query letters, payment vouchers for articles, rejection slips, etc.) that you can show the IRS to prove that you have been making bona fide professional efforts to sell material to the magazine.

To substantiate deducting magazines you purchase for research, you should be able to show an IRS auditor specific items/articles from the magazines and how you used them in your own work, such as query letters or articles you've written that relate directly to information presented in the magazines you have purchased for research information.

To substantiate deducting the magazines you purchase because you *think* you'd like to write for them, be able to show an auditor copies of correspondence (query letters, payment vouchers for articles, rejection slips, etc.) you have had with these magazines. If you deduct the cost of a magazine that you eventually find you are not interested in writing for, be able to show how and why you at first thought you might have been interested in writing for it. For instance, if your specialty is writing about horses, and you can document this to the IRS, then your one-time purchases of horse magazines that you do not write for will be deemed deductible if you can show that you were initially interested in writing for them.

In addition, you can deduct the writing-related costs of any newspapers, newsletters, reports, cassette tapes, etc., that you purchase or rent. For instance, if you're researching a book on investments, you may need to subscribe to some financial newspapers and newsletters. Again, be sure that you can substantiate your purpose for the subscriptions or purchases to the IRS.

Can you deduct the cost of books that you purchase related to your writing? Technically, anything that has a useful life of more than one year should be depreciated (see Chapter 8). Anything with a useful life of less than a year should be deducted. Thus, magazines are deductible, because it is assumed that their use will be limited to a short period of time (a month, etc.). You may be able to use books as references for many years, however. Here are some general rules to follow.

- If you purchase a book for limited use (such as for research for a piece you're writing), you can simply deduct the cost of the book.
- If the book you purchase is a relatively expensive reference item (one that you will refer to from time to time over the years), you should depreciate it.
- If you are building a library consisting of books of both kinds, you should *depreciate* all of your book purchases.
- If you purchase one or two relatively inexpensive books but have no other items that should be depreciated (typewriter, office furniture, home office, auto, etc.), it would be expedient simply to deduct their costs rather than go to the trouble of the whole depreciation process (bookkeeping, filling out depreciation forms, etc.).
- With the advent of "first year expensing," however (see Chapter 8), you may not have to be concerned with depreciation at all.

Again, the preceding discussion is based on the assumption that you are purchasing the books 100% for your writing business. If you are purchasing them partially for personal enjoyment and use (enjoyment outside of your writing business), you can deduct and/or depreciate *only* that percentage of the costs of the books that are related to your writing business.

EDUCATION

Depending on some specific factors, you may or may not be able to deduct expenses you incur for certain types of education.

You may deduct the ordinary and necessary expenses you have for education, even though the education may lead to a degree, if the education:

1) Is required by your employer, or by law or regulations, for keeping your salary, status, or job if the requirements are for a business purpose, or

2) Maintains or improves skills required in doing your present work.

You may not deduct expenses you have for education, even though the requirements are met, if the education is:

1) Required of you in order to meet the minimum educational requirements to qualify you in your work or business, or

2) Part of a program of study that will lead to qualifying you in a new trade or business.

You may not deduct the educational expenses that qualify you for a new trade or business even if you did not intend to enter that trade or business. [IRS Publication 508, *Educational Expenses*]

What does this mean to you as a writer? Here are some examples.

Example: You can deduct the cost of taking a writing course if you have already established yourself as a writer and are taking the course in order to improve your skills. You cannot deduct the cost of taking a writing course if you are not already a writer (i.e., if you have not already made some serious attempts to market your work and had some success in doing so).

Example: You can deduct the cost of a writer's conference if, again, you have established yourself as a freelance writer. You cannot deduct the cost of the conference if you are attending primarily to learn how to become a writer.

Example: You can deduct the cost of taking courses that will be of direct assistance in researching an article, articles, a book, or books that you are working on with the intent of selling. Be prepared, however, to substantiate that the course content is directly related to your research and is not simply for your pleasure or to help you obtain a new or different job. For instance, if you are writing an article or a book on tax law and take a course on tax law, the cost of that course is probably deductible. If, however, you continue to take law courses that lead to a law degree, the cost of that education is not deductible, because it qualifies you for a new profession (lawyer), even if you have no intention of ever taking the bar exam and practicing law.

If you follow the spirit of the law—that the courses you are taking help you become a better writer or researcher and do not qualify you for a new or different job (whether or not you plan to seek employment in that field)—your education costs will generally be considered deductible. If you are unsure about your specific situation, you may wish to consult an accountant or other tax professional.

Deductible Education Costs

If your education is deductible, you can deduct these expenses:

- tuition and fees
- books, supplies, lab fees, etc.
- tutoring
- travel and/or transportation

In general, all transportation and travel costs associated with your deductible education costs are deductible. This includes travel expenses to and from classes, meals and lodging if the course is away from home (such as a writer's conference in another city), and so on.

If part of your travel/transportation to and from educational programs or classes is devoted to personal pursuits, only that portion of your expenses that relates to your education is deductible. If you attend a convention in another city and spend a little bit of your spare time sightseeing, all your expenses are deductible (including travel and transportation) *except* those related to sightseeing. If you take a vacation in another city and happen to attend an educational program while on vacation, you may deduct only the expenses for the educational program but *not* travel and transportation costs to and from the other city, meals, lodging, etc. But if, for instance, you spend five days vacationing and stay for an extra day to attend an educational program, your lodging and meal expenses for that one day are deductible (assuming that the educational program is also deductible).

If you do deduct expenses for education, you may wish to attach an explanation of your deduction on a separate piece of paper and file it with your tax return. The explanation should include a description of the education and the purpose for which you took the program or course. This is optional, however. Doing so may either trigger or prevent an audit. If the IRS sees that you have claimed a deduction for education and included no explanation, it may be curious as to the validity of your claim. If you have included an explanation, however, and the IRS feels, as you do, that the expense was legitimate, it may pass you by for an audit. On the other hand, if you include an explanation that it does not agree with, the IRS may call you in to discuss it.

HOME OFFICE

For writers, the home office deduction is probably one of the most well known and most potentially economically valuable but also the most confusing. This section will help solve the puzzle by answering the following questions:

- Are you eligible to claim a home office deduction?
- If so, what limitations are there on the deduction?
- What expenses are actually deductible?
- How do you figure your total deduction?

Eligibility

Until 1976 the deduction was very easy to claim. In many cases, if you had a desk and chair in your den and spent some time working there, you could probably get away with claiming a home office deduction. As is true of any good thing, though, the deduction was abused. Employees who read business magazines in their living rooms in the evening claimed home office deductions. Investors who read stock reports at home claimed home office deductions for their dens. Writers who used a desk in the bedroom to write and sell one or two articles per year claimed home office deductions. "No more," said the IRS. Although interpretations seem to have liberalized a little in the past year or two, they are still extremely strict, eliminating almost every taxpayer. But one group of taxpayers that still has a good shot at legally claiming home office deductions is writers. Here is the basic law:

> [You can probably deduct] . . . any item to the extent such item is allocable to a portion of the dwelling unit which is *exclusively* used *on a regular basis—*
>
> (A) the *principal* place of business for any trade or business of the taxpayer,
>
> (B) as a place of business which is used by patients, clients, or customers in meeting or dealing with the taxpayer in the normal course of his trade or business, or
>
> (C) in the case of a separate structure which is not attached to the dwelling unit, in connection with the taxpayer's trade or business.
>
> [Italics added] [IRC Sec. 280A(c)(1)]

Before simplifying these guidelines and citing some examples, here are some definitions:

> *Exclusive use*—Exclusive use means that you must use a specific part of your home *only* for the purpose of carrying on your trade or business. If you use part of your home as your business office and also for personal purposes, you have not met the exclusive use test. [IRS Publication 587, *Business Use of Your Home*]

> *Regular use*—Regular use means that you use the exclusive business part of your home on a *continuing basis*. The occasional or incidental business use of a part of your home does not meet the regular use test even if that part of your home is

used for no other purpose. [IRS Publication 587, *Business Use of Your Home*]

Trade or business use—The business use of your home must be directly related to your trade or business. Use of your home for a profit-seeking activity that is not a trade or business does not allow you to take a deduction for business use of your home. [IRS Publication 587, *Business Use of Your Home*]

If you use the part of your home in question for both writing and nonwriting activities, you cannot claim a home office deduction.

Example: You write in the recreation room from 9:00 a.m. to 5:00 p.m. Your children play Ping-Pong or watch TV in the room in the evenings and/or on the weekends. No home office deduction is allowed. The room must be used *only* for your writing.

If you write occasionally, and the part of the home you use to write in is unused the rest of the time, you cannot claim a home office deduction.

Example: You have a typewriter, desk, and chair set up in a small room in your home. You spend a few days during the year writing a couple of articles. No home office deduction is permitted. You must use the room on a regular basis. (What is considered a regular basis, however, would have to be determined by an auditor, if you are audited, or a judge, if you take the matter to court.)

If you write for fun but every once in a while decide to generate some extra income, you will not be considered as engaging in a trade or business, even though it may be income-producing activity. You can take no home office deduction.

Example: If you are a housewife whose intent is to pick up a few extra dollars each year by writing, you will be ineligible for a home office deduction.

Example: If you are employed elsewhere for your primary income and write a few articles each year for sale, the IRS will probably hold that your primary trade or business is your other job, not writing. No home office deduction will be allowed. (In a couple of court cases, college professors who set aside areas of their homes for home offices in order to write articles were held ineligible to claim home office deductions, because writing was not their primary occupation.)

If you are a full-time professional writer with a home office but maintain your *main* office at some location other than your home, you may or may not be able to claim a home office deduction. If you use your other office most of the time, and your home office just occasionally, you probably *cannot* claim a home office deduction. If you regularly use both, but you use your home office more often, you probably *can* claim a home office deduction (proportional to the time you use your home office—see discussion below). Again, the home office must be considered your *principal* place of business.

Another gray area is what constitutes a "portion of the dwelling unit." If your home office is a separate room within the house, the answer is obvious. That room would be considered a legitimate "portion of the dwelling unit." What about a small section, area, or cubicle *within* a room? The judgments go both ways. If you have it partitioned off, you stand a good chance of claiming that section of the room as a legitimate home office. If it is not partitioned off, it is difficult to say. The IRS has ruled both ways. If you are not in doubt as to the validity of your claim, it might be advisable to enclose a photo of the portion of your home that you are claiming as a home office along with your tax return (clipped to Schedule C). If the IRS agrees with you that the portion is a valid home office, it may not bother to call you for an audit. If you do not enclose a photo, it may not audit you anyway, *or* it may be a little curious as to what you are calling a home office and call you for an audit.

Separate structures are treated slightly differently. Examples of separate structures are barns, studios, and garages not attached to the home. If you have such a structure that you use exclusively and regularly for your business, you may not have to meet the "principal place of business" rule. In other words, if you have two offices—one being a separate structure on your property at home and the other one being somewhere else, you can probably claim the separate structure as a home office, even if you use the other office more of the time for your writing. You must, however, still abide by the "regular" rule (you can't just use it once in a while) and the "exclusive" rule (you can't use it as a combination office/toolshed, for instance). The difference between a separate structure and part of your dwelling unit is this: If you work four days at a regular office and one day in a home office within your dwelling, the home office is not deductible, because it does not meet the "principal place of business" rule. However, if you work four days in a regular office and one day in a home office that is a separate structure from your home, the separate structure probably is deductible as a home office, because it is not bound by the "principal place of business" rule.

Limitations

The limitations on the home office deduction are determined by income, time, and space.

Income

The expenses you claim as a home office deduction may not exceed your writing income.

Example: Let's say you meet all the requirements of claiming a home office deduction. If you have annual expenses of $1,000 related to your home office, but you earn only $700 that year, you may deduct only $700 of your expenses, not the full $1,000.

Time

If you have two offices (a home office and another office) and legitimately claim a home office deduction, you can deduct expenses only in proportion to the amount of time you use your home office for writing.

Example: If you work four days a week in your home office and one day a week in another office, you can claim only four-fifths (4/5) of the expenses attributable to your home office. Thus, if you incurred $1,000 in home office expenses and worked in the office four days a week, you could claim a maximum of $800 (4/5 × $1,000) as a home office deduction.

Space

To determine what portion of your home expenses are attributable to your home office, you have to do some simple measuring and math. If your home has rooms of relatively equal size, and you use one of them as a home office, divide your expenses by the number of rooms in the house.

Example: If you have a 10-room house, one room of which is your office, you can deduct 10% of the allowable home expenses.

If you can't easily determine what percentage of your home is used for your home office, measure the area (square footage) of your home (all floors) and divide it by the area (square footage) of your home office.

Example: If you have a two-story home with a full basement, and a portion of your basement is used for a home office, your calculations might be something like this:

$$
\begin{array}{rl}
\text{First floor area:} & 1{,}200\ \text{ft}^2\ (30\ \text{ft} \times 40\ \text{ft}) \\
\text{Second floor area:} & 900\ \text{ft}^2\ (30\ \text{ft} \times 30\ \text{ft}) \\
\text{Basement area:} & 900\ \text{ft}^2\ (30\ \text{ft} \times 30\ \text{ft}) \\
\hline
\text{Total area:} & 3{,}000\ \text{ft}^2 \\
\end{array}
$$

Home office area: 500 ft² (25 ft × 20 ft)

500 ft² (divided by) 3,000 ft² (equals) one-sixth. Therefore, 1/6th (16.7%) of your allowable home expenses are deductible as home office expenses.

Deductible Expenses

For IRS purposes, deductible expenses fall into three classifications (the reason for which will be discussed shortly).

The first classification of home office expenses that you can deduct are those that you could deduct anyway if you claimed itemized personal deductions on Schedule A. These include mortgage interest payments and real estate taxes.

The second classification are all other expenses you incur related to your home office *except* depreciation. Such expenses include:

- *rent*—if you rent your dwelling rather than own it;
- *utilities*—gas, electric, water, trash, phone, etc.;
- *insurance*—homeowner's or renter's insurance;
- *miscellaneous*—maid service, light bulbs, cleaning supplies, etc.;

• *repairs*—patching walls, painting, etc.*

The third classification is depreciation expenses. Examples of depreciable expenses you might incur are the cost of rewiring, installing new plumbing, putting on a new roof, etc.

Note: Landscaping and lawn care expenses are *not* deductible or depreciable as home office expenses.

What percentages of deductible and depreciable expenses can you claim for home office deductions? In most cases this will be determined by the three limitations discussed above: income, time, and space.

> *Example:* If you earn $10,000 from writing, you have only one office (your home office), and your home office is 10% of your home's area, you can generally deduct (or depreciate) 10% of the expenses listed above (10% of your real estate taxes, 10% of your mortgage interest, 10% of your utilities, 10% of the cost of rewiring your home, etc.).

There are, however, some other considerations. If the expense does not benefit the home office in any way (such as repairing a wall in a bedroom), you may not deduct any of that expense as a home office expense.

If the expense benefits only your home office, you can deduct the whole amount, not just a percentage. If, for instance, you rented a carpet shampooer and shampooed only the carpet in your home office, you can deduct all of the cost (100%) of shampooing the carpet.

If you find that 50% of your trash is generated in your home office and 50% is generated in the rest of your home, you can probably deduct 50% of your trash pickup costs (instead of the percentage attributable to your home office by square footage). But if you do this, you will probably also be obligated to limit other utility expenses to actual costs. For instance, you would

---

*It is important to distinguish between *repairs,* which are generally direct expenses that can be deducted, and *improvements,* which are generally capital expenses that must be depreciated (see Chapter 8).

have to calculate the actual cost of heating and lighting your home office (excluding costs of operating your oven, washer/ dryer, etc.), and probably wouldn't be able to calculate this easily or accurately. In other words, it is probably advisable (and easier) simply to claim utility expenses in proportion to the square footage your home office occupies (limited, again, by income and time).

Why are home office expenses divided into the three classifications of personal deductions, business deductions, and depreciation? It has to do with the order in which you may deduct (or depreciate) your expenses. If you are claiming a home office, you must deduct expenses in the first classification first (interest and taxes) up to the limits placed on your deduction by income, time, and space.

> . . . the deductions allowed . . . for the taxable year by reason of being attributed to such use shall not exceed the excess of—
>
>   (A) the gross income derived from such use for the taxable year, over
>   (B) the deductions allocable to such use which are allowable under this chapter for the taxable year whether or not such unit (or portion thereof) was so used. [IRC Sec. 280A(c)(5)]

Next, if anything is left over, you can deduct expenses in the second classification (utilities, repairs, etc.).

Finally if there is *still* something left over, you can claim depreciation expenses third.

You cannot, in other words, claim depreciation as your first or second classification of expenses; nor can you claim business expenses as your first classification of expenses.

Example: Let's say that you earn $800 from writing and work exclusively in your home office. Let's also say that your expenses attributable to your home office are $1,000. The income limitation states that you cannot deduct the full $1,000. Only $800 of the $1,000 is deductible. Let's say the breakdown of your home office expenses is as follows:

Interest and taxes	$500
Additional expenses	$400
Depreciation	$100
Total Expenses	$1,000

To claim your $800, you must first deduct the $500 of interest and taxes, then the $300 of your $400 miscellaneous expenses. Since you have reached your $800 maximum, you cannot deduct the additional $100 of additional expenses or the $100 depreciation.

Why must you claim your expenses in this order? If you were able to claim depreciation expenses first, for instance, and then claim additional expenses second, and interest and taxes third, you would reach your $800 limit with $200 left over in the interest and taxes category. Since you weren't able to claim this $200 on your home office, you would be able to claim it on Schedule A as an itemized personal expense. You would, therefore, in other words, be able to claim the full $1,000 of expenses, even though you only had $800 income, and this is contrary to the IRS's requirements that home office expenses not exceed income.

Finally, if you are going to itemize personal deductions on Schedule A, remember to claim only the excess of your taxes and interest payments there, not the full amount.

Example: If you have $2,000 in taxes and interest deductions for the year and claim $200 of them for your home office on Schedule C, you can deduct *only* the excess ($1,800) as personal deductions on Schedule A.

What difference does it make where you deduct interest and taxes? By deducting them first on your home office you lower your taxable income and therefore the amount you are required to pay into Social Security. Second, if you are not claiming personal deductions on Schedule A (but instead claim the standard personal deduction), you of course cannot deduct any interest and taxes except what you deduct on Schedule C for your home office.

WORKSHEET 6: HOME OFFICE

Total area of home (square feet)   _4,000_

Total area of home office (square feet)   _400_

Percentage of area for home office   _10_ %
  (area of home office ÷ total area)

First Classification Expenses

Item	Total	(×)	%	(=)	Amt.
Mortgage Interest	$ _3,600_		_10_ %		$ _360.00_
Real Estate Taxes	$ _420_		_10_ %		+ $ _42.00_
Total					$ _402.00_

Second Classification Expenses

Item	Total	(×)	%	(=)	Amt.
Rent	$ _—_		_10_ %		$ _—_
Utilities					
Gas/Oil	$ _620_		_10_ %		$ _62.00_
Electricity	$ _425_		_10_ %		$ _42.50_
Water	$ _118_		_10_ %		$ _11.80_
Trash Removal	$ _75_		_10_ %		$ _7.50_
Insurance	$ _250_		_10_ %		$ _25.00_
Repairs	$ _—_		_10_ %		$ _—_
Misc. (maid service, cleaning, etc.)	$ _82_		_10_ %		$ _8.20_
Total					$ _157.00_

Third Classification Expenses

Item	Depreciable Amount
Depreciation on Office Itself (from Worksheet 7)	$ _360.00_
Depreciation on Improvements (based on percentage of value to home office; see Chapter 7)	$ _118.00_
Total	$ _478.00_
Total (all three classifications)	$ _1,037.00_

Figuring Your Total Deduction

For your convenience, there is a pull-out reproducible form in Appendix III of this book to help you calculate your home office deduction. Make copies of it and use it annually. But be sure to keep up with any changes in the law regarding home offices so you do not allow the form to become outdated.

INSURANCE

It is doubtful that you will have any insurance on your writing business per se. However, a discussion of some types of insurance you may have and how they might be related to your writing business should be helpful.

Health insurance premiums, while not deductible as business expenses on Schedule C, can often be deducted as personal expenses (medical deductions) on Schedule A if you itemize your personal deductions. I mention this because, as a writer, you may not be employed elsewhere and are probably paying for your own health insurance (instead of being covered under an employer's plan).

Auto insurance premiums are deductible to the extent that you use your vehicle for writing purposes and do not claim the standard mileage allowance (see "Car and Truck Expenses" in this chapter).

Homeowner's and renter's insurance premiums are partially deductible if you are claiming a home office deduction.

INTEREST

You can deduct interest that is related to your writing business, including interest on these items:

- a loan to purchase, for instance, office equipment
- oil company credit card purchases for writing-related vehicle expenses
- home mortgage payments (if you maintain a home office)
- credit card or revolving charge accounts for writing-related purchases.

If you fail to prepay your estimated income tax obligations (or underpay them), you will be charged an interest penalty by the IRS. These interest charges are *not* deductible (see Chapter 6).

Note: If you also itemize your personal deductions on Schedule A, you may *not* deduct interest twice.

Example: If you pay $100 in total interest in a year, $30 of which is writing-related, and you deduct this $30 as a business expense on Schedule C, you may deduct only the remaining $70 (not the whole $100) on Schedule A.

LEGAL AND PROFESSIONAL EXPENSES

If you engage the services of professionals in your writing business, you may deduct the fees you pay them. Such professionals would include the following.

- *lawyers,* who might, for instance, review book contracts for you
- *accountants,* who might help you with complex tax situations related to your writing
- *agents,* who might help you market your writing
- *proofreaders and other editorial consultants,* who might help you polish your work and make it more marketable
- *typists,* who handle occasional or regular typing/clerical jobs for you, assuming these people are not actually your employees
- *photographers,* who take photos for you to supplement your articles or books
- *cartoonists and illustrators,* who might illustrate your articles or books
- *messengers and messenger services*

OFFICE SUPPLIES AND POSTAGE

Postage that you purchase for your freelance writing business is deductible.

Generally, all other odds and ends you purchase for your writing business are deductible under "Office Supplies and Postage." Some of these are: paper, pens, pencils, erasers, staples, typewriter ribbon, personalized stationery, business cards, recording tape, envelopes, film, paper clips, and so on.

Such items as staplers, for instance, since they have a useful life of more than a year, should technically be depreciated. Since they are relatively inexpensive, however, you can claim them as simple deductions (especially with the advent of "first-year expensing"—see Chapter 8).

For office supplies such as office equipment/furniture (typewriters, desks, etc.), see Chapter 8.

RENT

Any rent you pay in relation to your writing business is deductible. For instance, if you rent a car while on a business trip, rent your residence (and claim a home office deduction), and/or rent equipment (typewriters, etc.), you can claim these expenses as rent expenses on Schedule C.

REPAIRS

Repairs per se are deductible. Improvements, however, must be depreciated. The difference? If the work significantly prolongs, increases, or extends the life of the item being worked on, you will probably have to depreciate it. If, however, the work is general maintenance, necessary to keep the item operating efficiently and to keep it from going into a state of major disrepair, and is of incidental cost, you can deduct it. See Chapter 8 for a full discussion of the difference.

Auto tune-ups, typewriter overhauls, and other similar jobs are generally considered deductible repair expenses. Expenses for major refurbishing of your home office, for instance, should probably be depreciated. If you aren't sure that you know whether a specific piece of work is a repair or an improvement, it might be wise to consult an accountant or other tax professional.

TAXES

Some taxes are deductible. Others are not. Here is a list of taxes you might encounter and how to treat them:

- *Federal income tax:* Not deductible.
- *Real estate tax:* Partially deductible if you maintain a home office.
- *Sales tax:* Technically, sales tax is deductible. However, since you probably include the sales tax you paid for writing-related purchases with the individual purchases, you cannot, of course, deduct it again. For instance, if you purchased $100 worth of office supplies in a state with a 5% sales tax, you would pay $105 for your purchase. The logical thing to do is deduct $105 for office supplies instead of deducting $100 for office supplies and $5 for taxes.
- *Social Security tax:* Not deductible.
- *Utility taxes:* Partially deductible if you maintain a home office. However, as with the discussion above on sales tax deductions, it makes more sense to deduct any utility expenses you incur in relation to your home office as utility expenses (instead of actual utility expenses plus additional taxes on the amounts). In other words, deduct the total amounts under the appropriate category rather than separate the tax portion from the main portion.

TRAVEL AND ENTERTAINMENT

This is a category that American taxpayers often get carried away with, deducting everything in sight that is remotely related to travel, entertainment, and gift giving. The IRS, of course, doesn't like it and often scrutinizes this category carefully when conducting audits.

As a writer, you can legally (and in good conscience) deduct certain travel, entertainment, and gift expenses that you incur.

> In general, there shall be allowed as a deduction all the *ordinary and necessary* expenses paid or incurred during the taxable year in carrying on any trade or business, including . . . traveling expenses (including amounts expended for meals and lodging *other than amounts which are lavish or extravagant* under the circumstances) while away from home *in the pursuit of a trade or business;* . . . [Italics added] [IRC Sec. 162(a)]

In general, *no deduction . . . shall be allowed* for any item . . . with respect to an activity which is of a type generally considered to constitute entertainment, amusement, or recreation, *unless* the taxpayer establishes that the item was *directly related to, . . .* the *active conduct of the taxpayer's trade or business, . . .* [Italics added] [IRC Sec. 274(a)(1)]

The IRS codes and regulations cover pages and, in the case of court decisions on travel and entertainment (T&E), volumes and volumes. For our purposes, there is no reason to go into any of these intricacies. Honesty and common sense are the two best tools you have here. If you legitimately and in good faith feel that your travel, entertainment, and gift expenses are (1) ordinary and necessary, (2) directly related and associated with the conduct of your business, and (3) not lavish or extravagant, you will proba-

bly be able to deduct them legally. You should, however, be able to prove the business worth and value of any and all expenses you claim for travel, entertainment, and gift giving. Let's look at them individually.

Travel

Generally, travel expenses are those you incur when you are engaged in your writing business away from home for a period of more than one day (general rule: overnight and/or when sleep is required). Travel expenses differ from transportation (car and truck) expenses in that transportation expenses generally refer to local, short-term (one day or less) driving. Examples of travel expenses, on the other hand, include the following.

- flying to another city for a three-day writing convention
- driving to another state for a week's research on an article or book you're writing
- a two-day trip to visit your editors in another city in order to collaborate on your book manuscript

What is deductible when you travel?

- transportation costs to and from your destination *and* in and around your destination while you are there (air fare, rail fare, bus fare, car rental, cab fare, etc.)
- meals and lodging while on the trip (hotel/motel room costs, restaurant expenses, etc.)
- incidental expenses (tips, baggage charges, cleaning/laundry expenses, phone expenses, etc.)

Is your trip a combination of business and pleasure? If your trip is primarily business and incidentally pleasure, you will be able to deduct all of your expenses *except* those expenses directly related to pleasure.

Example: If you attend a four-day writing convention in another city and stay for a fifth day to sightsee, you cannot deduct hotel/motel expenses for the extra day, nor can you deduct meals for that day, sightseeing expenses, etc.

If your trip is primarily pleasure and incidentally business, you *cannot* deduct any of your travel expenses *except* those directly related to business. You cannot, in other words, deduct transportation costs to and from your destination.

Example: If you take a four-day vacation in another city and stay for a fifth day to attend a convention, you can deduct hotel/motel expenses, meals, etc., for the fifth day *only*.

Use your good judgment and be able to substantiate your claims.

If a companion (spouse, employee, friend, etc.) travels with you, you may *not* deduct any of his or her expenses unless he or she is substantially important and necessary to your work. For instance, if your spouse is your full-time secretary or assistant in the regular and normal course of your writing, you can deduct his or her expenses when he or she travels with you for business purposes. If, on the other hand, your spouse does only incidental typing, note taking, etc., and is not necessary to the conduct of your business, his or her expenses are not deductible.

Keep a diary account whenever you travel. Your entries should always answer the following questions:

- Whom did you visit on your business trip (if anyone)?
- What was the business purpose of your trip?
- What business purpose did you actually accomplish?
- When did you leave and return?
- Where did you go?
- How did you get there (mode of transportation)?
- Where did you stay (hotel/motel, etc.)?
- How much did it all cost (separated by category)?

Keep receipts for all expenses over $25. Incidental expenses (those under $25) can generally be totaled and recorded without receipts.

Case: An attorney and his wife wrote a book about their travels around the world. They hoped to publish the book but did not. However, their primary purpose in taking the trip was for other reasons (sightseeing, visiting relatives, etc.). The court held that their expenses were not deductible. (Wright et al. v. Comm., 6 Cir; 1960.)

Entertainment

This is one of the most abused tax deductions the IRS allows. There is often a lot of room for honest differences of opinion between taxpayers and the IRS. Again, your best approach is to use common sense and good judgment. If you feel the entertainment costs you incur are directly and substantially related to your business, are ordinary and necessary, and are not lavish or extravagant, you should be able to deduct them.

The IRS codes, regulations, and court cases cover volumes; the intricacies, "loopholes," and ways to close the loopholes are more than most sane people can handle. If you are just looking for the simple and legitimate entertainment expense deductions, however, here is what you need to know:

Entertainment generally refers to business activities and meals; entertaining in social, athletic, and sporting clubs (if the clubs are used primarily for business entertaining); entertaining business associates at theaters, sporting events, etc.; expenses you incur if a business associate visits and stays with you (cost of meals you serve, etc.) or if you foot the bill for the guest to stay at a local hotel/motel, etc.

Here are some examples of how writers might entertain:

- You set up an interview with a person for an article you are writing and arrange to meet for lunch to conduct the interview. If you pay for the lunch, that is an entertainment expense.
- You take your editor(s) to dinner and a ball game, during which time you discuss new article ideas you have. If you foot the bill, the expenses are legitimate entertainment expenses.
- If you are writing a feature story on "life in the nightclubs" in your city, all of your legitimate expenses associated with

your research at the clubs you attend are deductible. (If you don't sell the piece, however, you should be able to substantiate that you had reasonable cause to believe the piece was saleable.)

But if you're on a business trip and spend your evenings in a nightclub just to relax after work, those expenses are not deductible.

Again, make comprehensive and regular diary entries or other records of your entertainment expenses and keep all receipts for amounts over $25. List and answer the following questions.

- Whom did you discuss business with during the entertainment (name and title)?
- What business did you discuss?
- Where did you entertain (name and address of the facility)?
- When did the entertainment occur?
- What were the associated costs (itemized)?

Gifts

You may engage in some gift giving of one sort or another as a writer. For instance, if you send Christmas cards to your editors, all of the costs associated with these are deductible as gift expenses.

The general IRS rule for gifts is that they must be directly related to your business and not cost more than $25 for each individual. If you present an editor with a $40 Christmas gift, you may deduct only $25 of that.

Note: It has nothing to do with taxes, but many people in the field of journalism/publishing are not allowed to accept gifts, particularly in the newspaper field. Christmas cards, of course, are almost always acceptable. You might want to find out ahead of time (discreetly) what a particular publication's policy is toward having their editors and others accept gifts.

Keep records of gifts you give:

- What did you give as a gift?
- To whom (name and title)?

- For what reason?
- When was it given?
- What did it cost?

UTILITIES AND TELEPHONE

If you maintain an office for your writing business (home office or otherwise), you may deduct part of your utilities, with certain limitations.

If you use your telephone in your writing business, you may deduct that portion that is related to your writing. In other words, if you use your phone half for personal use and half for business use, you may deduct half the cost of the purchase, installation, and maintenance of your phone; half of your monthly service charges; etc. *All* of the costs of long-distance calls you make related to your writing are deductible.

If you maintain a separate telephone line exclusively for your writing, *all* of the costs associated with that telephone are deductible.

If you make calls away from home that are related to your writing, you may want to charge them to your home number and deduct them as they appear on your monthly bill. If, however, you choose to pay for the calls in cash, keep records of the calls and deduct them either under "Travel and Entertainment" or "Utilities and Telephone."

WAGES

Under most circumstances, as a freelance writer, you will not be hiring employees to work for you. On occasion you may procure the services of a secretary/typist or other support personnel. In general, this can be considered a "Legal and Professional" expense, since this person is probably self-employed and is not legally your employee.

If, however, you have a family and utilize the services of one or more members (husband, wife, child, etc.) and pay them for their work, they are probably going to be considered employees. In this case you can deduct the amounts you pay them under "Wages" on Schedule C.

This can, however, be very complex for a couple of reasons. The first and obvious reason is that you are now an employer and as such are governed by myriad complex laws, regulations, and requirements. You will probably have to withhold taxes and Social Security from their wages and file special reports and returns to the IRS, which can be a real headache. The second reason is that the IRS frowns on family employee situations. Why? Many people abuse the option and use it as a tax shelter. They pay outrageously high wages to their children for small (or no) amounts of work to reduce their own taxable income. The children, of course, are taxed at a much lower rate. The children return the money to the parent (or the parent may not even actually pay it in the first place), and a bundle is saved in taxes.

Bottom line: If you really do utilize the services of one or more family members to assist you in your writing business, if they really do provide valuable services, and if you are willing to actually (and irretrievably) pay them reasonable wages for their work, you can deduct such expenses from your income. However, it is recommended that you get in touch with an accountant or other tax professional to determine how to set yourself up as a bona fide employer.

MISCELLANEOUS EXPENSES

The "Miscellaneous" expense line on Schedule C is there in order to let you list any expenses you incur that are not listed elsewhere on the schedule. Education expenses, for instance, should be listed here. Here are some other miscellaneous expenses you might incur as a writer:

- *photographs* that you purchase from a person, photo service, newspaper, or other source for use with your articles and/or books. (If the amount is negligible, you can probably report them under "Office Supplies and Postage.") The same is true for photo developing expenses.
- *safe deposit box* (if you maintain one for the sole purpose of protecting your manuscripts, business records, and other materials).
- *duplication* (copying and duplication costs).

A FINAL WORD ON DEDUCTIONS

You will undoubtedly (probably inevitably) come across some expenses that seem to fit logically into more than one IRS category (as listed on Schedule C). Where should you report them? Basically, wherever you want. Choose the most logical category, if there is one. If not, flip a coin.

Here are some examples of expenses that fit into more than one category:

Expense	*Possible Categories*
flyers to advertise your writing class	"Advertising" "Miscellaneous" (copying expenses)
automobile insurance	"Car and Truck Expenses" "Insurance"
entertaining your lawyer	"Travel and Entertainment" "Legal and Professional"
car rental	"Car and Truck Expenses" "Rent"
safe deposit box	"Rent" "Miscellaneous"
business calls from phone booth in another city	"Utilities and Telephone" "Travel and Entertainment"
travel to writing conference	"Travel and Entertainment" "Miscellaneous" (education expenses)
books for writing class	"Dues and Publications" "Miscellaneous" (education expenses)

Finally, the home office deduction does not have a specific IRS category on Schedule C. Home office expenses should be claimed, then, in the appropriate individual categories:

Claim	Under
mortgage interest	"Interest"
real estate taxes	"Taxes"
repairs	"Repairs"
trash removal	"Utilities and Telephone"
electric, gas, water, etc.	"Utilities and Telephone"
rent	"Rent"
insurance	"Insurance"
misc. (cleaning, etc.)	"Other Expenses"

8

Depreciation

There are some expenses you may incur as a writer that cannot simply be deducted. They must be depreciated. Generally, these are assets (items) that have a useful life of more than a year.

If you buy business property that has a useful life of more than one year, you cannot deduct its cost as an expense when you figure your business income for tax purposes. Instead, you must spread the cost over more than one year, and deduct it a portion at a time. This is called depreciation. [IRS Publication 534, *Depreciation*]

Property is depreciable if it meets these requirements:
1) It must be used in business or held for the production of income.
2) It must have a useful life that can be determined, and its useful life must be longer than one year. . . .
3) It must be something that wears out, decays, gets used

up, becomes obsolete, or loses value from natural
causes. [IRS Publication 534, *Depreciation*]

Depreciable property is classified as either *real* property or
personal property. Real property is anything that is erected on
land (your home office, for instance).

If you rent, you cannot claim depreciation on your home office,
since you don't own the structure. The owner of the structure will
be the one who claims depreciation.

Personal property, generally, is everything else that is depreciable. Some depreciable personal property you might have as a
freelance writer would be:

adding machine	professional library
files	calculator
tape recorder	copy machine
typewriter	home computer
office furniture	automobile (unless you claim
word processor	the standard mileage
camera	allowance; see Chapter 7)

Note: Since you can't claim depreciation on nonbusiness assets,
you must determine the appropriate percentage of business use
for an asset and claim only that percentage for depreciation.

Example: If you use your vehicle for writing purposes 40% of
the time and for personal use 60% of the time, you can claim
only 40% of the total depreciation on the vehicle.

REPAIRS VERSUS IMPROVEMENTS

Should you depreciate or deduct repairs and improvements? In
general, you should deduct repairs and depreciate improvements
(see Chapter 7 for additional discussion). You do, however, need
to determine which work is considered repair and which is considered improvement.

Repairs and replacements. You may deduct the cost of repairs
and replacements that do not increase the value of property,

make it more useful, or lengthen its useful life. However, if a repair or replacement increases the value of the property, makes it more useful, or lengthens its life, you must capitalize and depreciate these costs. You cannot deduct these costs. [IRS Publication 534, *Depreciation*]

What you spend to keep your property in a normal, efficient, operating condition is a deductible expense. But if what you spend adds to the value of your property or significantly increases its life, the cost must be capitalized. [IRS Publication 535, *Business Expenses*]

Repairs do not add to the value or usefulness of property, nor do they appreciably lengthen its life. They merely maintain the property in a normal efficient operating condition. They do not extend its estimated useful life or change the purpose for which it was acquired. The cost of repairs, . . . is a deductible expense. [IRS Publication 535, *Business Expenses*]

Improvements add to the value of property, lengthen its life, or adapt it to a different use. The cost of an improvement . . . may not be deducted in full as a current expense. [IRS Publication 535, *Business Expenses*]

The theory behind it all is that, if the work benefits you over the years and is major, it is an improvement, and you should depreciate it over the years. If you benefit only now and/or the work is minor, it is a repair, and you can deduct it now.

Example: If you patch a leak in the wall, that is considered a temporary and minor repair. It is deductible. If, however, you add a new roof to your home, that is a major, long-term improvement and is therefore depreciable.

What repairs and improvements might you encounter as a freelance writer?

- *Home office repairs:* painting, patching, etc.
- *Home office improvements:* rewiring, replumbing, new floor, new roof, etc.

- *Auto repairs:* general repairs (leaky radiator, etc.)
- *Auto improvements:* engine overhauls, etc.
- *Equipment repairs:* general repairs (broken key on typewriter, etc.)
- *Equipment improvements:* adding desk space, library space, etc.

CLAIMING DEPRECIATION

With each year, it seems, depreciation gets easier and easier to compute and more economically appealing. Prior to 1981 there were a number of different and relatively complex types of depreciation in existence: straight line, declining balance, sum of the years' digits, CLADR, etc. Since 1981, however, a new type of depreciation has gone into effect: Accelerated Cost Recovery System (ACRS); and as of 1982, if your depreciable personal property (but not real property) assets cost less than $5,000, you have the option of simply claiming the total amount as a simple deduction through what is called "first-year expensing," which will be explained at length later in this chapter.

Where do your assets fit in? Which type of depreciation can (or must) you use? Generally, you must use the method(s) of depreciation in effect in the year you placed your asset into service of any kind (not necessarily business service). However, depreciation itself begins in the year you placed your asset into business service.

> *Placed in service.* Property is considered placed in service when it is in a condition or state of readiness and availability for a specifically assigned function whether in a trade or business, in the production of income, in a tax-exempt activity, or in a personal activity. Depreciation begins when the property is first ready for service in a trade or business or for the production of income. [IRS Publication 534, *Depreciation*]

Confusing? The following examples should help clarify things.

Example: If you purchase a typewriter in 1981 and begin

using it for writing in the same year, you must use the method of depreciation in effect in 1981 (ACRS); your first year of actual depreciation is also 1981.

Example: If you purchased a car in 1980, used it for personal driving for a year, and began using it for your writing business in 1981, you must use a method of depreciation in effect in 1980 (miscellaneous methods, but not ACRS); your first year of actual depreciation is 1981.

Example: If you buy a home in 1975 and convert one room into a home office in 1982, you must use a method of depreciation in effect in 1975 (miscellaneous methods, but not ACRS); your first year of actual depreciation on the home office is 1982.

It is important to understand the distinction between *method of depreciation* and *first year of depreciation. Method of depreciation* is the way you will depreciate the asset (the system used), such as straight line method, ACRS method, etc. *First year of depreciation* is the first of the "x" number of years you actually will be claiming depreciation (3 years, 5 years, 10 years, etc.).

The value of the asset when you place it into use is not necessarily the same as the purchase price, especially if you place the asset into service a few years later.

Example: Let's say you buy a car in 1980 for $4,000 for personal use. You become a writer in 1982 and begin using your car for writing purposes in 1982. In 1982 the car is worth, say, $2,000. The amount you can use for depreciation purposes is $2,000 then, not $4,000.

What if you hadn't heard of (or used) depreciation until now? What method do you use and when is your first year of depreciation? Quite simply, the rules are the same. It doesn't matter when you become aware of your right to claim depreciation.

Example: Let's say you bought a home in 1975 and converted one room into a home office in 1982, but you didn't become aware of depreciation until 1983. Thus, 1983 will be the first year you will claim depreciation on your tax return. To claim depreciation you must use a method of depreciation that was in effect in 1975, and your first year of depreciation will be 1982. Thus, in 1983 you will actually be claiming the percentage of depreciation allowable for your second year of depreciation. If you wish to claim depreciation for 1982, the year you missed, you must file an amended tax return (1040-X).

In other words, whether you claimed depreciation in the past or not does not change the status of your depreciable assets at all.

DEPRECIATION PRIOR TO ACRS (PRIOR TO 1981)

If you placed any depreciable assets into service prior to 1981 and have been using any of the depreciation methods in effect at that time (straight line, declining balance, sum of the years digits, CLADR, etc.), continue to use this method over the life of your assets.

If you placed any assets into service prior to 1981 and have *not* been depreciating them, you should see an accountant or other tax professional if you wish to begin depreciating them. Why? Again, you must use one of the old methods of depreciation, and they can be quite difficult to understand and complicated to utilize.

ACRS DEPRECIATION

Beginning in 1981, as part of the Economic Recovery Act of 1981, a new type of simplified and accelerated depreciation was introduced: ACRS (Accelerated Cost Recovery System). It is a blessing—sweet and simple!

Beginning in 1981, everything that you placed into service that is depreciable must be depreciated using ACRS. All depreciable assets, as far as you will be concerned as a freelance writer, will fall into four categories:

• Automobiles and small trucks: 3-year property

- Office equipment, furniture, and fixtures: 5-year property
- Mobile homes (for home office purposes): 10-year property
- Regular homes (for home office purposes): 15-year property

It is easier to discuss the 3-, 5-, and 10-year property separately from the 15-year property. To figure depreciation on 3-, 5-, and 10-year property under ACRS, simply determine the value of the asset and use the percentages in the following table [source: IRS Publication 534, *Depreciation*].

Year	3-year property	5-year property	10-year property
1	25%	15%	8%
2	38%	22%	14%
3	37%	21%	12%
4		21%	10%
5		21%	10%
6			10%
7			9%
8			9%
9			9%
10	____	____	9%
	100%	100%	100%

Note: The percentages in this table are in effect for ACRS property placed in service in 1981-1984. For percentages in effect for property placed in service after 1984, see Appendix I.

Here is an example of how you would depreciate your assets using ACRS:

Example: If you purchased an electronic typewriter (five-year property) for $2,000 in 1982, you would claim depreciation like this:

$$
\begin{array}{llll}
\text{1982 (1st year)} & 15\% \times \$2,000 = & \$300 \\
\text{1983 (2nd year)} & 22\% \times \$2,000 = & \$440 \\
\text{1984 (3rd year)} & 21\% \times \$2,000 = & \$420 \\
\text{1985 (4th year)} & 21\% \times \$2,000 = & \$420 \\
\text{1986 (5th year)} & 21\% \times \$2,000 = & \underline{\$420} \\
& & \$2,000
\end{array}
$$

If you are planning to claim ACRS depreciation on the automobile you use for your writing business, you may not use the standard mileage allowance in any year(s) *prior* to claiming ACRS depreciation. In other words, if you purchased a car in 1981 and claimed the standard mileage allowance that year, you could choose to claim individual expenses the following year, but you could not include depreciation as part of those individual expenses. However, if you started out by claiming individual expenses (including depreciation), you are free to switch to the standard mileage allowance rate in years after that, but you may not then again claim depreciation if you return to claiming individual expenses in later years (see Chapter 7). Also, if you use ACRS depreciation on your auto, your automobile will be fully depreciated after three years (because it is classified as three-year property under ACRS rules), and you must use the mileage allowance in effect for fully depreciated automobiles if you claim the standard mileage allowance in the fourth (or later) year(s).

Depreciating 15-year property is a little different. Unlike 3-, 5-, and 10-year property, you must take into consideration the month you placed the 15-year property into service when claiming ACRS depreciation. To determine the allowable percentages of depreciation for your home office, use the table at the top of page 101 [source: IRS Publication 534, *Depreciation*].

Here is how you would claim depreciation for your home office if it is classified as 15-year real property under ACRS:

Example: If you placed your home office into service in

15-year Real Property Table *(other than low-income housing)*

Year	(Use the Column for the Month in the First Year the Property Is Placed in Service)											
	1	2	3	4	5	6	7	8	9	10	11	12
1st	12%	11%	10%	9%	8%	7%	6%	5%	4%	3%	2%	1%
2d	10%	10%	11%	11%	11%	11%	11%	11%	11%	11%	11%	12%
3d	9%	9%	9%	9%	10%	10%	10%	10%	10%	10%	10%	10%
4th	8%	8%	8%	8%	8%	8%	9%	9%	9%	9%	9%	9%
5th	7%	7%	7%	7%	7%	7%	8%	8%	8%	8%	8%	8%
6th	6%	6%	6%	6%	7%	7%	7%	7%	7%	7%	7%	7%
7th	6%	6%	6%	6%	6%	6%	6%	6%	6%	6%	6%	6%
8th	6%	6%	6%	6%	6%	6%	5%	6%	6%	6%	6%	6%
9th	6%	6%	6%	6%	5%	6%	5%	5%	5%	6%	6%	6%
10th	5%	6%	5%	6%	5%	5%	5%	5%	5%	5%	6%	5%
11th	5%	5%	5%	5%	5%	5%	5%	5%	5%	5%	5%	5%
12th	5%	5%	5%	5%	5%	5%	5%	5%	5%	5%	5%	5%
13th	5%	5%	5%	5%	5%	5%	5%	5%	5%	5%	5%	5%
14th	5%	5%	5%	5%	5%	5%	5%	5%	5%	5%	5%	5%
15th	5%	5%	5%	5%	5%	5%	5%	5%	5%	5%	5%	5%
16th	—	—	1%	1%	2%	2%	3%	3%	4%	4%	4%	5%

March, go to Column 3 on the chart above (which represents March, the third month). Moving down the column to Year 1, you see that you can claim a depreciation expense of 10%. In the second year you could claim a depreciation expense of 11%, 9% in the third year, etc., all the way to 1% the 16th year.

Each column adds up to 100%, in other words. It's just a matter of which month of the year you place your home office into service that determines how the percentages are distributed each year.

With any type of depreciation (ACRS or otherwise), the value of the land is always subtracted first before computing any depreciation.

Example: If your home cost $50,000 and the land value is estimated at $10,000, you would use the figure $40,000 as the basis for computing depreciation. In other words, if your home office was 10% of the square footage of your home, you would be able to depreciate $4,000 ($40,000 × 10%), not $5,000 ($50,000 × 10%) for your home office.

Let's say, then, that you have a $4,000 depreciable home office, and you placed it into service in March 1982. Here are the depreciation amounts you would claim:

1982	(Year)	1	10% × $4,000 =	$400
1983		2	11% × $4,000 =	$440
1984		3	9% × $4,000 =	$360
1985		4	8% × $4,000 =	$320
1986		5	7% × $4,000 =	$280
1987		6	6% × $4,000 =	$240
1988		7	6% × $4,000 =	$240
1989		8	6% × $4,000 =	$240
1990		9	6% × $4,000 =	$240
1991		10	5% × $4,000 =	$200
1992		11	5% × $4,000 =	$200
1993		12	5% × $4,000 =	$200
1994		13	5% × $4,000 =	$200
1995		14	5% × $4,000 =	$200
1996		15	5% × $4,000 =	$200
1997		16	1% × $4,000 =	$ 40
			100%	$4,000

Note: See Appendix III for sample forms for recording pertinent information on depreciable assets.

Optional Straight-Line ACRS Election

If you wish, you can depreciate ACRS property over a greater number of years using the ACRS Straight-Line Election method. You may depreciate:

3-year property over 3, 5, or 12 years
5-year property over 5, 12, or 25 years
10-year property over 10, 25, or 35 years
15-year property over 15, 35, or 45 years

To figure depreciation by this method, simply determine the number of years you wish to depreciate the asset over and use the following table:

3-year election: 33.333% per year
5-year election: 20.000% per year
10-year election: 10.000% per year
12-year election: 8.333% per year
15-year election: 6.666% per year
25-year election: 4.000% per year
35-year election: 2.857% per year
45-year election: 2.222% per year

There is a "half-year convention" rule for 3-, 5-, and 10-year property if you use the optional method. You can claim only one-half (½) of the yearly depreciation the first year, regardless of the month you placed the asset into service. You then claim the other one-half in the year following the last year of depreciation.

Example: If you chose to depreciate your $2,000 electronic typewriter (5-year ACRS property) over five years using the optional method, here is how it would compare with the regular method:

Year	ACRS		Optional ACRS	
1	15% × $2,000 = $300		10% × $2,000 = $200 *	
2	22% × $2,000 = $440		20% × $2,000 = $400	
3	21% × $2,000 = $420		20% × $2,000 = $400	
4	21% × $2,000 = $420		20% × $2,000 = $400	
5	21% × $2,000 = $420		20% × $2,000 = $400	
6	_____	_____	10% × $2,000 = $200	
	100%	$2,000	100%	$2,000

* = half-year convention

On 3-, 5-, and 10-year property, if you choose the optional method for one asset, you must also depreciate in the same way all other assets in that classification that were placed into service in the same year.

Example: Let's say you placed your typewriter (five-year property) into service in 1981 and chose the optional ACRS method to depreciate it. If you also placed a tape recorder (also five-year property) into service in the same year, you would have to depreciate the tape recorder using the optional method as well. You could not use the regular method for one and not the other. However, if you placed the tape recorder into service in 1982 (a different year), you would have your choice of how to depreciate it (ACRS or optional ACRS). If you placed an automobile (three-year property) into service in 1981 (the same year you placed your typewriter into service) and chose to use the optional method for the typewriter, you would still have your choice of methods (ACRS or optional ACRS) for the automobile, since it is a different classification of property (three-year) than the typewriter (five-year).

Regular versus Optional ACRS

Which ACRS depreciation method is better for you: regular ACRS or optional ACRS? Ask yourself the following questions:

• How long will you be writing?
• How many useful years will you get out of each asset?

You should determine what you feel to be the useful life of the asset you're going to depreciate and depreciate it over the number of years closest to that (or over fewer years). You can't depreciate something you're not using, so you wouldn't want to depreciate an asset over a longer period of time than you'll be using it. If you want maximum depreciation allowances early, choose the least number of years available. If you want depreciation spread out over the years, choose the number of years closest to what you consider the useful life.

WORKSHEET 7: DEPRECIABLE ASSETS

Item	Home Office		Typewriter		Automobile					
Placed in Service	March 1981		1982		1983					
Type of Depreciation	ACRS		ACRS		Optional ACRS					
Value	$4,000		$2,000		$4,500					
Life	15 years		5 years		5 years					
Year	%	$	%	$	%	$	%	$	%	$
1981	10	$400								
1982	11	$440	15	$300						
1983	9	$360	22	$440	10	$450				
1984	8	$320	21	$420	20	$900				
1985	7	$280	21	$420	20	$900				
1986	6	$240	21	$420	20	$900				
1987	6	$240			20	$900				
1988	6	$240			10	$450				
1989	6	$240								
1990	5	$200								
1991	5	$200								
1992	5	$200								
1993	5	$200								
1994	5	$200								
1995	5	$200								
1996	1	$40								
1997										
1998										
1999										
2000										
Total	100	$4,000	100	$2,000	100	$4,500				

Example: If you're 50 years old, you wouldn't want to depreciate your home office over 45 years, unless you plan to be writing when you're 95.

Example: If you're thinking of depreciating your typewriter over 12 years instead of the standard five, will you actually be using that typewriter in 12 years? If not, you'll lose money, because you can't depreciate something you're not using.

Once you claim one method of depreciation, you generally cannot switch back and forth. The rules are complex here. For some methods you can switch from one to another without special IRS permission. For other types you cannot switch—ever. If you feel a need (or desire) to switch, see an accountant or other tax professional.

FIRST-YEAR EXPENSING

First-year expensing is another real blessing for freelance writers. As of 1982 items that you could normally deduct only through depreciation can now (in certain cases) simply be deducted. This means, in other words, that you can claim the whole amount of the deduction in one year instead of having to spread it out over a number of years (as required by depreciation). This applies to personal property (not real property, such as a home office) that would be eligible for an investment credit (discussed later in this chapter).

In 1982 and 1983 you can deduct up to $5,000 ($2,500 for married persons filing separate returns) of your otherwise depreciable purchases as simple expenses. (For future rates, see Appendix I.)

Example: If you purchase a $2,000 electronic typewriter in 1983, you don't have to depreciate it. You may simply claim a $2,000 deduction.

Example: If you purchase a $7,000 word processor in 1983, however, you can deduct only $5,000 and depreciate the remaining $2,000 (using regular ACRS or optional ACRS).

If you claim first-year expensing on otherwise depreciable assets, *you may not also claim an investment credit* (see section below).

Example: Assume the same situation as in the above example. If you chose to claim the $5,000 first-year expensing and depreciated only the remaining $2,000, you could claim an investment credit on *only* the $2,000, *not* the total $7,000.

Remember, the total amount (for 1982 and 1983) must not exceed $5,000.

Example: If, in 1983, you purchased a $2,000 typewriter, a $500 camera, $2,000 worth of office furniture, and a $1,000 duplicating machine (total value $5,500) for your writing business, you could deduct $5,000 and claim the remaining $500 as a depreciation expense (and also claim a $500 investment credit).

INVESTMENT CREDIT

In a nutshell, most of the depreciable assets you purchase for your writing business (whether new or used) qualify for an investment credit of 10%. An investment credit allows you actually to deduct 10% of the purchase price of depreciable business assets *directly from your tax liability,* not from your income.

Example: If you find you owe $500 in tax (before you figure any investment credit), and you have purchased a $5,000 office machine, you can claim a $500 investment credit on that machine. As a result, you owe no tax at all ($500 – $500 = $0)!

Assets defined as three-year property under ACRS, such as your automobile, are eligible for only a 6% investment credit.

Example: Let's say you purchase an automobile for $5,000

and use it 100% for your writing business. Before figuring any tax credits, you find you owe a total of $400 in income tax on Form 1040. Your investment credit for the automobile is $300 ($5,000 × 6%). Subtract the $300 credit from the $400 tax; thus, you owe only $100 in tax.

Assets defined as five-year property under ACRS, such as office equipment, furniture, etc., are eligible for the 10% investment credit.

Bottom line: The IRS is actually footing a percentage of your depreciable asset purchases. If you are eligible for a 10% credit on a $2,000 purchase, you are actually paying only $1,800. The IRS is paying the other $200. (On top of this, you can also claim depreciation, so the IRS is paying even more; i.e., letting you pay less.)

As with everything else, you must figure any investment credit based on the percentage of *business* use your assets have. In other words, if you use your car 50% for business and 50% for pleasure, you get only half the available credit on the full value of the car:

Cost of car: $5,000
Business use: 50%
Cost available for credit: $2,500
Investment credit allowed: 6%
Investment credit amount: $150 ($2,500 × 6%)

Even though you cannot claim ACRS depreciation on your automobile if you claim the standard mileage allowance (see Chapter 7), you can claim an investment credit on it. You do not have to claim individual auto expenses in order to claim an investment credit.

Your investment credit cannot exceed the total amount of tax you owe in a year. In other words, if you owe $500 in taxes but have an investment credit of $600, you cannot claim the full $600 credit and expect the government to refund you $100. If your investment credit exceeds your tax, there are special ways to report this. It is recommended that you see an accountant or other tax professional. (There are also many other types of credits available to taxpayers in general: energy credit, credit for the elderly, child care credit, etc. Since they are not directly related to freelance writing, they will not be discussed here. However, if you will be claiming any of them, remember that the total of your tax credits—all types of credits—may not exceed the amount of tax you owe in a year. Again, see an accountant or other tax professional to claim your excess credits.)

You can claim an investment credit only once for any given asset, not each and every year. In other words, if you purchase a typewriter in 1983 and claim an investment credit of 10% on the typewriter in 1983, you cannot claim another 10% in 1984. Claim investment credits in the year you purchase an asset and place it into service.

Buildings in general are excluded from eligibility for investment credits. Bottom line: Your home office (whether in a regular home, condominium, mobile home, or apartment) is not eligible for an investment credit.

The investment credit and first-year expensing are certainly economic boons to freelance writers. However, remember that you cannot claim both on the same asset. In other words, if you buy a $2,000 electronic typewriter, you can either (1) expense the whole $2,000 and claim it as a deduction in one year or (2) depreciate it over its five-year recovery property (under ACRS) and claim the 10% investment credit, but not both. Which option is best for you? One is not always better than the other. It depends on the value of the asset you purchase, its useful life, your current income, and your income in the years to come. To determine which option is best for you, you need to do some individual estimating and calculating.

Example: Let's say you purchase a $2,000 electronic typewriter in 1983. You estimate your total income for the next four years in Column A. Column B lists your taxes if you claim ACRS five-year depreciation and the investment credit. Column C lists your taxes if you claim first-year expensing.

Year	A	B		C	
		Expense	*Tax*	*Expense*	*Tax*
1983	$10,000	$300	$ 1,200	$2,000 =	$ 860
1984	$12,000	$440	$ 1,500	—	$ 1,600
1985	$14,000	$420	$ 2,000	—	$ 2,000
1986	$16,000	$420	$ 2,400	—	$ 2,600
1987	$18,000	$420	$ 3,000	—	$ 3,000
			$10,100		$10,600
			− $ 200*		
			$ 9,900		

* = first year investment credit

Results indicate that in strict dollars saved, claiming the depreciation and first-year investment credit would be the better option, but remember that 1987 dollars will not be 1983 dollars in terms of inflation, interest, etc. You may be able to invest your first year's savings realized by first-year expensing at a rate of interest that would offset later years' higher tax rates for first-year expensing. Another consideration is the tax rate itself. The tax due on the amounts listed is based on the 1983 tax rate, which may go up, down, or remain the same in later years. Because so many uncontrollable and unknown factors are involved—how much you'll be earning, the tax rate, inflation, interest, etc.—it is literally impossible to figure out now what the better option is in any one case. My own personal choice is first-year expensing. I take what I can get when I can get it and deal with the future when it arrives. However, you may be "built" differently than I am, and you may like to make an "investment for the future" of sorts by claiming depreciation and first-year investment credit. An accountant or other tax professional may be able to steer you in the right direction based on your specific financial situation. If not, though, it's a toss-up.

Part III

Filing Your Tax Returns

Now, step by step, we'll fill out your tax form. Copies of sample tax returns are included so you can follow these examples. The forms being used are for the 1982 tax year (payable in 1983), so your current year's forms may be slightly different. In general, though, the forms remain largely the same from year to year.

You will definitely need:

- *Form 1040:* "U.S. Individual Income Tax Return" (long form)
- Schedule C: "Profit (or Loss) From Business or Profession"

You will probably need:

- *Schedule SE:* "Computation of Social Security Self-Employment Tax" (see Chapter 5)

You *may* need:

- *Form 1040-ES:* "Declaration of Estimated Tax for Individuals" (see Chapter 6)
- *Form 2210:* "Underpayment of Estimated Tax by Individuals" (see Chapter 6)
- *Form 3468:* "Computation of Investment Credit" (see Chapter 8)
- *Form 4562:* "Depreciation and Amortization" (see Chapter 8)

Based on the references in the text, determine which form(s) and schedule(s) you will need to complete your tax return. Then follow the appropriate steps below. The steps included apply to the forms and schedules described above. Each step has in parentheses the number or letter of the form or schedule being discussed in the step. If and when you reach a step that refers to a form or schedule you are not required to use, simply skip the step and proceed to the next one.

First, however, let's set the scenario. For illustrative purposes, we'll use a fictitious freelance writer, Fred E. Lance. Fred is single and lives at a home on 2100 Maple St., Maple City, IL 60000. Fred received the first Social Security number ever issued: 000-00-0000. When not laboring over his first love, writing, Fred is a dutiful employee at a meat-packing plant, where he earned $15,000 in wages in 1982 and had federal income taxes of $2,800 withheld.

But on to more interesting things—Fred's writing income and expenses. In 1982 Fred sold the following articles:

Magazine A	$100
Magazine B	$300
Magazine C	$800
Magazine D	$800
Total	$2,000

Most of his income, however, came from business newsletters he wrote, for which publishers paid him $8,000. His total writing income: $10,000.

It cost Fred quite a bit to earn that $10,000:

Bank service charges	$ 8.00
Car and truck expenses	$682.00

Dues and publications	$118.00
Legal and professional services	$ 50.00
Office supplies and postage	$551.00
Travel and entertainment	$136.00
Educational program	$119.00
Photos	$ 18.00
Copying	$ 42.00

Fred also maintained a home office. His percentage of total home expenses for his home office gave these totals:

Insurance	$ 47.00
Mortgage interest	$360.00
Real estate taxes	$ 42.00
Utilities and telephone	$285.00

He bought his home and placed his home office into service in July 1981. His home cost $40,000; his home office is 10% of the home, so the depreciable value of his home office is $4,000.

In 1982, Fred also purchased $1,500 worth of office furniture and a $2,000 electronic typewriter.

STEP 1 (FORM 4562)

A. Fred filled in his name, business activity, and Social Security number at the top.
B. He decided to claim first-year expensing on his office furniture and entered it in Part I, Section A.
C. He decided to claim ACRS depreciation on his typewriter and listed it in Section B, Line 2b (five-year property). The appropriate deduction for the first year on five-year property is 15%; thus he can claim $300 this year.
D. He began depreciating his home office in 1981 and continues to do so in 1982. He enters the appropriate information on Line 2f.
E. His total for Section B is entered on Line 4.
F. His totals for the complete form are entered appropriately on Lines 8, 9, and 10.
G. Fred enters the amount from Line 10 also on Schedule C, Line 12.

| Form **4562** (Rev. September 1982) Department of the Treasury Internal Revenue Service (0) | **Depreciation and Amortization** ▶ See separate instructions. ▶ Attach this form to your return. | OMB No. 1545–0172 Expires 8/31/85 **67** |

Name(s) as shown on return   Fred E. Lance

Identifying number   000 - 00 - 0000

Business or activity to which this form relates   Writer

Part I   Depreciation

Section A   Election to expense recovery property (Section 179)

A. Class of property	B. Cost	C. Expense deduction
Office furniture (5-year)	$1,500 —	$1,500 —

1 Total (not more than $5,000). Enter here and on line 8 (Partnerships—enter this amount on Schedule K (Form 1065)) . . . . $1,500 —

Section B   Depreciation of recovery property

A. Class of property	B. Date placed in service	C. Cost or other basis	D. Recovery period	E. Method of figuring depreciation	F. Percentage	G. Deduction for this year
2 Accelerated Cost Recovery System (ACRS) (See instructions):						
(a) 3-year property						
	1982	$2,000 —	5 yr.	ACRS	15%	$300 —
(b) 5-year property						
(c) 10-year property						
(d) 15-year public utility property						
(e) 15-year real property—low-income housing						
	July 1981	$4,000 —	15 yr.	ACRS	11%	$440 —
(f) 15-year real property other than low-income housing						
3 Property subject to section 168(e)(2) election (See instructions):						

4 Total column G. Enter here and on line 9 . . . . $740 —

See Paperwork Reduction Act Notice on page 1 of the separate instructions.   Form **4562** (Rev. 9–82)

Form 4562 (Rev. 9–82)   Page **2**

Section C   Depreciation of nonrecovery property

A. Description of property	B. Date acquired	C. Cost or other basis	D. Depreciation allowed or allowable in earlier years	E. Method of figuring depreciation	F. Life or rate	G. Deduction for this year
5 Class Life Asset Depreciation Range (CLADR) System Depreciation . . . . ▶						
6 Other depreciation (See instructions):						

7 Total column G, Section C . . . .

8 Enter amount from Section A, line 1 (Partnerships enter zero) . . . . $1,500 —

9 Enter amount from Section B, line 4 . . . . $740 —

10 Total—Add lines 7, 8, and 9. Enter here and on the Depreciation line of your return . . . . $2,240 —

Part II   Amortization of property

A. Description of property	B. Date acquired	C. Cost or other basis	D. Amortization allowed or allowable in earlier years	E. Code section	F. Amortization period or percentage	G. Amortization for this year

Total column G. Enter here and on Other deduction or expense line of your return . . . .

STEP 2 (SCHEDULE C)

A. Fred again fills his name, occupation, and Social Security number in at the top, as well as his address.
B. He checks the "Cash" box in "Accounting Method," as well as "Yes" to questions on home office (H), business operation (I), and number of months operating his business (J).
C. He enters his total writing income in Part I.
D. He lists his expenses in Part II.
E. On Line 31 he enters his total expenses.
F. On Line 32 he subtracts Line 31 (total expenses) from Line 5 (total income), and enters his net profit from writing.

SCHEDULE C (Form 1040) Department of the Treasury Internal Revenue Service (O)	**Profit or (Loss) From Business or Profession** (Sole Proprietorship) Partnerships, Joint Ventures, etc., Must File Form 1065. ▶ Attach to Form 1040 or Form 1041. ▶ See Instructions for Schedule C (Form 1040).	OMB. No. 1545–0074 **1982** 08

Name of proprietor   Fred E. Lance   **Social security number of proprietor** 000 00 0000

A Main business activity (see Instructions) ▶ Writer   ; product ▶

B Business name ▶ —

C Employer identification number

D Business address (number and street) ▶ 2100 Maple St.
    City, State and ZIP Code ▶ Maple City, IL 60000

E Accounting method: (1) ☒ Cash   (2) ☐ Accrual   (3) ☐ Other (specify) ▶

F Method(s) used to value closing inventory:
   (1) ☐ Cost   (2) ☐ Lower of cost or market   (3) ☐ Other (if other, attach explanation)

	Yes	No
G Was there any major change in determining quantities, costs, or valuations between opening and closing inventory? . . If "Yes," attach explanation.		X
H Did you deduct expenses for an office in your home?		X
I Did you operate this business at the end of 1982?		X

J How many months in 1982 did you actively operate this business? ▶ 12

Part I   Income

1 **a** Gross receipts or sales	**1a**	$10,000	—
b Returns and allowances	**1b**		
c Balance (subtract line 1b from line 1a)	**1c**	$10,000	—
2 Cost of goods sold and/or operations (Schedule C–1, line 8)	**2**		
3 Gross profit (subtract line 2 from line 1c)	**3**	$10,000	—
4 **a** Windfall Profit Tax Credit or Refund received in 1982 (see Instructions) . .	**4a**		
b Other income	**4b**		
5 Total income (add lines 3, 4a, and 4b) . . . . ▶	**5**	$10,000	—

Part II   Deductions

6 Advertising			25 Taxes (Do not include Windfall Profit Tax here. See line 29.) . .	$42	—
7 Bad debts from sales or services (Cash method taxpayers, see Instructions)			26 Travel and entertainment . .	$136	—
			27 Utilities and telephone . .	$285	—
8 Bank service charges	$8	—	28 **a** Wages . .		
9 Car and truck expenses	$682	—	**b** Jobs credit		
10 Commissions			**c** Subtract line 28b from 28a .		
11 Depletion			29 Windfall Profit Tax withheld in 1982		
12 Depreciation, including Section 179 expense deduction (from Form 4562)	$2,240	—	30 Other expenses (specify):		
13 Dues and publications	$118	—	**a** Education program	$119	—
14 Employee benefit programs . .			**b** Photos	$18	—
15 Freight (not included on Schedule C–1) .			**c** Copying	$42	—
16 Insurance	$47	—	**d**		
17 Interest on business indebtedness	$360	—	**e**		
18 Laundry and cleaning			**f**		
19 Legal and professional services .	$50	—	**g**		
20 Office supplies and postage . .	$551	—	**h**		
21 Pension and profit-sharing plans .			**i**		
22 Rent on business property . . .			**j**		
23 Repairs			**k**		
24 Supplies (not included on Schedule C–1) .			**l**		
			m		

31 **Total deductions** (add amounts in columns for lines 6 through 30m) . . . . ▶	**31**	$4,698	—
32 Net profit or (loss) (subtract line 31 from line 5). If a profit, enter on Form 1040, line 12, and on Schedule SE, Part I, line 2 (or Form 1041, line 6). If a loss, go on to line 33	**32**	$5,302	—

33 If you have a loss, do you have amounts for which you are not "at risk" in this business (see Instructions)? . . ☐ Yes   ☐ No
If you checked "No," enter the loss on Form 1040, line 12, and on Schedule SE, Part I, line 2 (or Form 1041, line 6).

For Paperwork Reduction Act Notice, see Form 1040 Instructions.

Schedule C (Form 1040) 1982   Page 2

SCHEDULE C–1.—Cost of Goods Sold and/or Operations (See Schedule C Instructions for Part I, line 2)

1 Inventory at beginning of year (if different from last year's closing inventory, attach explanation) .	**1**	
2 Purchases (less cost of items withdrawn for personal use)	**2**	
3 Cost of labor (do not include salary paid to yourself)	**3**	
4 Materials and supplies	**4**	
5 Other costs	**5**	
6 Add lines 1 through 5	**6**	
7 Inventory at end of year	**7**	
8 Cost of goods sold and/or operations (subtract line 7 from line 6). Enter here and on Part I, line 2 . ▶	**8**	

☆U.S.GPO:1982-0-363-310   E.I.# 430614328

STEP 3 (SCHEDULE SE)

    A. Fred enters his name and Social Security number at the top.

    B. He then enters his net profit from writing (Schedule C, Line 32) on Line 2.

    C. He enters this amount again on Lines 8 and 9.

    D. He enters the amount from Line 10 again on Line 12.

    E. He compares the amounts on Lines 9 and 12 and enters the smaller of the two on Line 13.

    F. He multiplies this amount by the appropriate amount (.0935)* and enters the total on Line 14.

---

*Remember that this amount will be increasing in future years. See Appendix I.

| SCHEDULE SE (Form 1040) Department of the Treasury Internal Revenue Service (0) | **Computation of Social Security Self-Employment Tax** ▶ See Instructions for Schedule SE (Form 1040). ▶ Attach to Form 1040. | OMB No. 1545–0074 **1982** 22 |

| Name of self-employed person (as shown on social security card) Fred E. Lance | Social security number of self-employed person ▶ 000 00 0000 |

Part I   **Regular Computation of Net Earnings from Self-Employment**

1	Net profit or (loss) from Schedule F (Form 1040), line 57 or line 90, and farm partnerships, Schedule K–1 (Form 1065), line 18b **1**	
2	Net profit or (loss) from Schedule C (Form 1040), line 32, and Schedule K–1 (Form 1065), line 18b (other than farming). See instructions for kinds of income to report. **Note:** If you are exempt from self-employment tax on your earnings as a minister, member of a religious order, or Christian Science practitioner because you filed Form 4361, check here ▶ ☐. If you have other earnings of $400 or more that are subject to self-employment tax, include those earnings on this line **2**	$5,302 —

Part II   **Optional Computation of Net Earnings from Self-Employment**

Generally, this part may be used only if:
- Your gross farm profits were not more than $2,400, or
- Your gross farm profits were more than $2,400 and your net farm profits were less than $1,600, or
- Your net nonfarm profits were less than $1,600 and less than two-thirds (⅔) of your gross nonfarm income.

See instructions for other limitations.

3	Maximum income for optional methods	**3**	$1,600 00
4	Farm Optional Method—Enter two-thirds (⅔) of gross profits from Schedule F (Form 1040), line 31 or line 88, and farm partnerships, Schedule K–1 (Form 1065), line 18a, or $1,600, whichever is smaller	**4**	
5	Subtract line 4 from line 3 . . . . , . .	**5**	
6	Nonfarm Optional Method—Enter the smaller of two-thirds (⅔) of gross profits from Schedule C (Form 1040), line 3, and Schedule K–1 (Form 1065), line 18c (other than farming), $1,600, or, if you elected the farm optional method, the amount on line 5	**6**	

Part III   **Computation of Social Security Self-Employment Tax**   **SE**

7	Enter the amount from Part I, line 1, or, if you elected the farm optional method, Part II, line 4 . .	**7**	
8	Enter the amount from Part I, line 2, or, if you elected the nonfarm optional method, Part II, line 6 .	**8**	$5,302 —
9	Add lines 7 and 8. If less than $400, you are not subject to self-employment tax. Do not fill in the rest of the schedule	**9**	$5,302 —
10	The largest amount of combined wages and self-employment earnings subject to social security or railroad retirement tax for 1982 is	**10**	$32,400 00
11 a	Total FICA wages from Forms W–2 and RRTA compensation . . **11a**		
b	Unreported tips subject to FICA tax from Form 4137, line 9, or to RRTA tax **11b**		
c	Add lines 11a and 11b	**11c**	— —
12	Subtract line 11c from line 10	**12**	$32,400 —
13	Enter the smaller of line 9 or line 12	**13**	$5,302 —
	If line 13 is $32,400, fill in $3,029.40 on line 14. Otherwise, multiply line 13 by .0935 and enter the result on line 14		.0935
14	Self-employment tax. Enter this amount on Form 1040, line 51	**14**	$496 —

For Paperwork Reduction Act Notice, see Form 1040 Instructions.

☆U.S.GPO:1982-0-363-326   E.I.# 430814326

STEP 4 (FORM 1040)

A. Fred again fills in his name, address, Social Security number, and occupation at the top.
B. He checks Filing Status Box 1 ("Single") and claims himself as an exemption on Line 6a and again on 6e.
C. He enters his wages from the meat-packing plant on Line 7.
D. He enters his net writing profit on Line 12 (from Schedule C, Line 32).
E. Fred totals Lines 7 and 12 and enters the amount on Line 22.
F. He again enters this amount on Line 32 and Line 33.
G. He enters his exemptions (× $1,000) on Line 36.
H. He then enters his taxable income on Line 37.
I. He finds his tax from the Tax Table and enters it on Line 38 and again on Line 40.
J. Fred temporarily lays Form 1040 aside in order to compute his investment credit on his electronic typewriter.

Form **1040**	Department of the Treasury—Internal Revenue Service **U.S. Individual Income Tax Return** **1982**		(0)

For the year January 1–December 31, 1982, or other tax year beginning _____ 1982, ending ____ 19__ | OMB No. 1545-0074

Use IRS label. Other-wise, please print or type.	Your first name and initial (if joint return, also give spouse's name and initial) **Fred E.**	Last name **Lance**	Your social security number **000 00 0000**
	Present home address (Number and street, including apartment number, or rural route) **2100 Maple St.**		Spouse's social security no.
	City, town or post office, State and ZIP code **Maple City, IL 60000**	Your occupation ▶ **Writer** Spouse's occupation ▶	

Presidential Election Campaign
Do you want $1 to go to this fund? . . . . | Yes | No
If joint return, does your spouse want $1 to go to this fund? . . . | Yes | No

Note: Checking "Yes" will not increase your tax or re duce your refund.

Filing Status
Check only one box.

1. ⊠ Single
2. ☐ Married filing joint return (even if only one had income)
3. ☐ Married filing separate return. Enter spouse's social security no. above and full name here ▶ _____
4. ☐ Head of household (with qualifying person). (See page 6 of Instructions.) If the qualifying person is your un married child but not your dependent, enter child's name ▶
5. ☐ Qualifying widow(er) with dependent child (Year spouse died ▶ 19__). (See page 6 of Instructions.)

For Privacy Act and Paperwork Reduction Act Notice, see Instructions

Exemptions
Always check the box labeled Yourself. Check other boxes if they apply.

6a ⊠ Yourself ☐ 65 or over ☐ Blind
b ☐ Spouse ☐ 65 or over ☐ Blind
Enter number of boxes checked on 6a and b ▶ **1**

c First names of your dependent children who lived with you ▶ _____
Enter number of children listed on 6c ▶

d Other dependents:

(1) Name	(2) Relationship	(3) Number of months lived in your home	(4) Did dependent have income of $1,000 or more?	(5) Did you provide more than one-half of dependent's support?

Enter number of other dependents ▶

e Total number of exemptions claimed . . . .
Add numbers entered in boxes above ▶ **1**

Income
Please attach Copy B of your Forms W–2 here.
If you do not have a W–2, see page 5 of Instructions.

7	Wages, salaries, tips, etc.	7	$15,000
8	Interest income (attach Schedule B if over $400 or you have any All-Savers interest)	8	
9a	Dividends (attach Schedule B if over $400)_____, 9b Exclusion_____		
c	Subtract line 9b from line 9a	9c	
10	Refunds of State and local income taxes (do not enter an amount unless you de-ducted those taxes in an earlier year—see page 9 of Instructions)	10	
11	Alimony received	11	
12	Business income or (loss) (attach Schedule C) . . . . ▶	12	$5,302
13	Capital gain or (loss) (attach Schedule D)	13	
14	40% capital gain distributions not reported on line 13 (See page 9 of Instructions)	14	
15	Supplemental gains or (losses) (attach Form 4797)	15	
16	Fully taxable pensions, IRA distributions, and annuities not reported on line 17 . .	16	
17a	Other pensions and annuities. Total received ▶ 17a		
b	Taxable amount, if any, from worksheet on page 10 of Instructions	17b	
18	Rents, royalties, partnerships, estates, trusts, etc. (attach Schedule E)	18	
19	Farm income or (loss) (attach Schedule F) . . . . ▶	19	
20a	Unemployment compensation (insurance). Total received ▶ 20a		
b	Taxable amount, if any, from worksheet on page 10 of Instructions	20b	
21	Other income (state nature and source—see page 10 of Instructions) ▶ _____	21	
22	**Total income.** Add amounts in column for lines 7 through 21 . . . . ▶	22	$20,302

Please attach check or money order here.

Adjustments to Income
(See Instruc-tions on page 11)

23	Moving expense (attach Form 3903 or 3903F) . . .	23	
24	Employee business expenses (attach Form 2106) . .	24	
25	Payments to an IRA. You must enter code from page 11 (____)	25	
26	Payments to a Keogh (H.R. 10) retirement plan . . .	26	
27	Penalty on early withdrawal of savings	27	
28	Alimony paid	28	
29	Deduction for a married couple when both work (at-tach Schedule W)	29	
30	Disability income exclusion (attach Form 2440) . . .	30	
31	**Total adjustments.** Add lines 23 through 30 . . . . ▶	31	

Adjusted Gross Income

32	**Adjusted gross income.** Subtract line 31 from line 22. If this line is less than $10,000, see "Earned Income Credit" (line 62) on page 15 of Instructions. If you want IRS to figure your tax, see page 3 of Instructions . . . . ▶	32	$20,302

⬥ U.S. GOVERNMENT PRINTING OFFICE: 1982-363-301 E.I. 43-0787287

Form 1040 (1982)   Page **2**

Tax Computation (See Instructions on page 12)	33 Amount from line 32 *(adjusted gross income)*	33	$20,302 —
	34a If you itemize, complete Schedule A (Form 1040) and enter the amount from Schedule A, line 30	34a	
	Caution: If you have unearned income and can be claimed as a dependent on your parent's return, check here ▶ ☐ and see page 12 of the Instructions. Also see page 12 of the Instructions if: ● You are married filing a separate return and your spouse itemizes deductions, OR ● You file Form 4563, OR ● You are a dual-status alien.		
	34b If you do not itemize, complete the worksheet on page 13. Then enter the allowable part of your charitable contributions here	34b	
	35 Subtract line 34a or 34b, whichever applies, from line 33	35	
	36 Multiply $1,000 by the total number of exemptions claimed on Form 1040, line 6e . .	36	$1,000 —
	37 Taxable Income. Subtract line 36 from line 35	37	$19,302 —
	38 Tax. Enter tax here and check if from ☐ Tax Table, ☐ Tax Rate Schedule X, Y, or Z, or ☐ Schedule G	38	$3,543 —
	39 Additional Taxes. (See page 13 of Instructions.) Enter here and check if from ☐ Form 4970, ☐ Form 4972, ☐ Form 5544, or ☐ section 72 penalty taxes . . . . }	39	
	40 Total. Add lines 38 and 39 . . . . ▶	40	$3,543 —
Credits (See Instructions on page 13)	41 Credit for the elderly *(attach Schedules R&RP)*	41		
	42 Foreign tax credit *(attach Form 1116)*	42		
	43 Investment credit *(attach Form 3468)*	43	$200 —	
	44 Partial credit for political contributions	44		
	45 Credit for child and dependent care expenses *(attach Form 2441)* .	45		
	46 Jobs credit *(attach Form 5884)*	46		
	47 Residential energy credit *(attach Form 5695)*	47		
	48 Other credits—see page 14 ▶	48		
	49 Total credits. Add lines 41 through 48	49	$200 —
	50 Balance. Subtract line 49 from line 40 and enter difference (but not less than zero) . ▶	50	$3,343 —
Other Taxes (Including Advance EIC Payments)	51 Self-employment tax *(attach Schedule SE)*	51	$496 —
	52 Minimum tax *(attach Form 4625)*	52	
	53 Alternative minimum tax *(attach Form 6251)*	53	
	54 Tax from recapture of investment credit *(attach Form 4255)*	54	
	55 Social security (FICA) tax on tip income not reported to employer *(attach Form 4137)* .	55	
	56 Uncollected employee FICA and RRTA tax on tips *(from Form W-2)*	56	
	57 Tax on an IRA *(attach Form 5329)*	57	
	58 Advance earned income credit (EIC) payments received *(from Form W-2)*	58	
06	59 Total tax. Add lines 50 through 58 . . . . ■	59	$3,839 —
Payments Attach Forms W-2, W-2G, and W-2P to front.	60 Total Federal income tax withheld	60	$2,800 —	
	61 1982 estimated tax payments and amount applied from 1981 return .	61	$ 800 —	
	62 Earned income credit. If line 33 is under $10,000, see page 15 of Instructions	62		
	63 Amount paid with Form 4868	63		
	64 Excess FICA and RRTA tax withheld (two or more employers) .	64		
	65 Credit for Federal tax on special fuels and oils *(attach Form 4136)*	65		
	66 Regulated Investment Company credit *(attach Form 2439)*	66		
	67 Total. Add lines 60 through 66 . . . . ▶	67	$3,600 —
Refund or Amount You Owe	68 If line 67 is larger than line 59, enter amount OVERPAID . . . . ▶	68	
	69 Amount of line 68 to be REFUNDED TO YOU . . . . ▶	69	
	70 Amount of line 68 to be applied to your 1983 estimated tax . . . ▶	70	
	71 If line 59 is larger than line 67, enter AMOUNT YOU OWE. Attach check or money order for full amount payable to Internal Revenue Service. Write your social security number and "1982 Form 1040" on it. ▶ $ (Check ▶ ☐ if Form 2210 (2210F) is attached. See page 16 of Instructions.) ▶ $	71	$239 —
Please Sign Here	Under penalties of perjury, I declare that I have examined this return, including accompanying schedules and statements, and to the best of my knowledge and belief, it is true, correct, and complete. Declaration of preparer (other than taxpayer) is based on all information of which preparer has any knowledge.		
	▶ *Fred E. Lance*	4/15/83	
	Your signature Date	▶ Spouse's signature (if filing jointly, BOTH must sign)	
Paid Preparer's Use Only	Preparer's signature ▶	Date	Check if self-employed ▶ ☐	Preparer's social security no.
	Firm's name (or yours, if self-employed) and address ▶		E.I. No. ▶ ZIP code ▶	

STEP 5 (FORM 3468)

A. Fred enters his name and Social Security number at the top.

B. He enters the cost of his typewriter on Line 1b, Column 2; multiplies the amount by 100%; and enters the amount again on Line 1b, Column 4.

C. He enters the amount again on Line 5.

D. He multiplies the amount by the 10% allowable investment credit and enters the appropriate amount on Line 8, Line 14, and Line 17.

E. He refers back to Form 1040, Line 38, and enters this amount on Form 3468, Lines 18, 20, 21a, and 22.

F. He compares the amounts on Lines 17 and 22 and enters the smaller of the two on Line 23 and again on Line 27.

STEP 6 (FORM 1040)

A. Fred again returns to Form 1040 and enters the amount from Form 3468, Line 27, on Form 1040, Lines 43 and 49.

B. On Line 50 Fred enters Line 40 minus Line 49.

C. He enters the amount from Schedule SE, Line 14, on Form 1040, Line 51.

D. Fred adds Lines 50 and 51 and enters the total on Line 59.

E. He enters the $2,800 he had withheld from his meat-packing job on Line 60.

F. During 1982 Fred made estimated tax payments of $800 (four equal payments of $200 each). He enters this amount on line 61.

G. He enters the total of Lines 60 and 61 on Line 67.

H. Since Line 59 is larger than Line 67, Fred enters the difference on Line 71, the additional amount he owes.

I. Fred signs the return and dates it.

Form **3468**	**Computation of Investment Credit**		OMB No. 1545-0155
Department of the Treasury Internal Revenue Service (0)	▶ Attach to your tax return. ▶ Schedule B (Business Energy Investment Credit) on back.		**1982** 27

Name(s) as shown on return	Fred E. Lance	Identifying number 000-00-0000

PART I.— Elections

A The corporation elects the basic or basic and matching employee plan percentage under section 48(n)(1) . . . . . ☐
B i elect to increase my qualified investment to 100% for certain commuter highway vehicles under section 46(c)(6) . . ☐
C I elect to increase my qualified investment by all qualified progress expenditures made this and all later tax years. . . . ☐
  Enter total qualified progress expenditures included in column (4), Part II ▶ _____
D I claim full credit on certain ships under section 46(g)(3) (See Instruction B for details.) . . . . ☐

PART II.—Qualified Investment

1 Recovery Property		Line	(1) Class of Property	(2) Unadjusted Basis	(3) Applicable Percentage	(4) Qualified Investment (Column 2 × column 3)
Regular Percentage	New Property	(a)	3-year		60	
		(b)	Other	$2,000—	100	$2,000—
	Used Property	(c)	3-year		60	
		(d)	Other		100	
§48(q) Election to Reduce Credit (instead of adjusting basis) FY 1982–83 filers only (see instr.)	New Property	(e)	3-year		40	
		(f)	Other		80	
	Used Property	(g)	3-year		40	
		(h)	Other		80	

2 Nonrecovery property—Enter total qualified investment (See instructions for line 2) .	**2**		
3 New commuter highway vehicle—Enter total qualified investment (See Instruction D(2)) .	**3**		
4 Used commuter highway vehicle—Enter total qualified investment (See Instruction D(2)) .	**4**		
5 Total qualified investment in 10% property—Add lines 1(a) through 1(h), 2, 3, and 4 (See instructions for special limits)	**5**		$2,000—
6 Qualified rehabilitation expenditures—Enter total qualified investment for:			
a 30-year-old buildings	**6a**		
b 40-year-old buildings	**6b**		
c Certified historic structures (Enter the Dept. of Interior assigned project number _____)	**6c**		
7 Corporations checking election box A above—add lines 5, 6a, 6b, and 6c .	**7**		

PART III.—Tentative Regular Investment Credit

8 10% of line 5	**8**	$200—
9 15% of line 6a	**9**	
10 20% of line 6b	**10**	
11 25% of line 6c	**11**	
12 Corporations checking election box A (See Instruction D(1))—		
a Basic 1% credit—Enter 1% of line 7 (1982–83 fiscal-year filers, see instructions for line 12) . . .	**12a**	
b Matching credit (not more than 0.5%)—Allowable percentage times adjusted line 7 (attach schedule) .	**12b**	
13 Credit from cooperative—Enter regular investment credit from cooperatives	**13**	
14 Current year regular investment credit—Add lines 8 through 13	**14**	$200—
15 Carryover of unused credits	**15**	
16 Carryback of unused credits	**16**	
17 Tentative regular investment credit—Add lines 14, 15, and 16	**17**	$200—

PART IV.—Tax Liability Limitations

18 a Individuals—From Form 1040, enter tax from line 38, page 2, plus any additional taxes from Form 4970 b Estates and trusts—From Form 1041, enter tax from line 26a, plus any section 644 tax on trusts . c Corporations (1120 filers)—From Form 1120, Schedule J, enter tax from line 3 . d Other organizations—Enter tax before credits from return	**18**	$3,543—
19 a Individuals—From Form 1040, enter credits from lines 41 and 42 of page 2 . . b Estates and trusts—From Form 1041, enter any foreign tax credit from line 27a . c Corporations (1120 filers)—From Form 1120, Schedule J, enter any foreign tax credit from line 4(a), plus any possessions tax credit from line 4(f) . . . . . d Other organizations—Enter any foreign or possessions tax credit	**19**	—
20 Income tax liability as adjusted (subtract line 19 from line 18)	**20**	$3,543—
21 a Enter smaller of line 20 or $25,000. See instruction for line 21	**21a**	$3,543—
b If line 20 is more than $25,000—Enter 90% of the excess	**21b**	
22 Regular investment credit limitation—Add lines 21a and 21b	**22**	$3,543—
23 Allowed regular investment credit—Enter the smaller of line 17 or line 22 . .	**23**	$200—
24 Business energy investment credit limitation—Subtract line 23 from line 20 . .	**24**	
25 Business energy investment credit—From line 14 of Schedule B (Form 3468) . .	**25**	
26 Allowed business energy investment credit—Enter smaller of line 24 or line 25 .	**26**	
27 Total allowed regular and business energy investment credit—Add lines 23 and 26. Enter here and on Form 1040, line 43; Schedule J (Form 1120), line 4(b), page 3; or the proper line on other returns .	**27**	$200—

For Paperwork Reduction Act Notice, see separate instructions.

Form **3468** (1982)

Form 3468 (1982)   Page **2**

Schedule B   Business Energy Investment Credit

1 Enter on lines 1(a) through 1(e) your qualified investment in business energy property that is the kind listed in the instructions for line 1, column (3).

(1) Type of Property	Line	(2) Class of property or life years	(3) Code	(4) Unadjusted basis/ Basis	(5) Applicable Percentage	(6) Qualified investment (Column 4 × column 5)
Recovery	(a)	3-year			60	
	(b)	Other			100	
Nonrecovery	(c)	3 or more but less than 5			33⅓	
	(d)	5 or more but less than 7			66⅔	
	(e)	7 or more			100	

2 Total 10% energy investment property—Add lines 1(a) through 1(e), column (6) . . | **2** |

3 Enter on lines 3(a) through 3(e) the basis in qualified hydroelectric generating property. Enter nameplate capacity of the property (see instructions for line 3) ▶

(1) Type of Property	Line	(2) Class of property or life years	(3) Code	(4) Unadjusted basis/ Basis	(5) Applicable Percentage	(6) Qualified investment
Recovery	(a)	3-year			60	
	(b)	Other			100	
Nonrecovery	(c)	3 or more but less than 5			33⅓	
	(d)	5 or more but less than 7			66⅔	
	(e)	7 or more			100	

4 Total 11% energy investment property—Add lines 3(a) through 3(e), column (6) . . | **4** |

5 Enter on lines 5(a) through 5(e) the basis in energy property that is solar equipment, wind equipment, ocean thermal equipment, or geothermal equipment. (See instructions for line 5, column (3).)

(1) Type of Property	Line	(2) Class of property or life years	(3) Code	(4) Unadjusted basis/ Basis	(5) Applicable Percentage	(6) Qualified investment
Recovery	(a)	3-year			60	
	(b)	Other			100	
Nonrecovery	(c)	3 or more but less than 5			33⅓	
	(d)	5 or more but less than 7			66⅔	
	(e)	7 or more			100	

6 Total 15% energy investment property—Add lines 5(a) through 5(e), column (6) . . | **6** |
7 Enter 10% of line 2 . . . . | **7** |
8 Enter 11% of line 4 . . . . | **8** |
9 Enter 15% of line 6 . . . . | **9** |
10 Cooperative credit—Enter business energy investment credit from cooperatives . . . | **10** |
11 Current year business energy investment credit—Add lines 7 through 10 . . . . . | **11** |
12 Carryover of unused credit(s) . . . . | **12** |
13 Carryback of unused credit(s) . . . . | **13** |
14 Tentative business energy investment credit—Add lines 11 through 13. Enter here and on line 25 of Form 3468 . . . . | **14** |

Instructions for Schedule B (Form 3468)

Energy property must meet the same requirements as regular investment credit property, except that the provisions of sections 48(a)(1) and 48(a)(3) do not apply. See Instructions for Form 3468 for definitions and rules regarding regular investment credit property.

Energy property must be acquired new. See sections 46(a)(2)(C) and 48(l)(1) through (17) for definitions.

See section 48(l)(17) for special rules on public utility property, and section 48 (l)(11) (as amended by the Crude Oil Windfall Profit Tax Act of 1980) for special rules on property financed by Industrial Development Bonds.

Specific Instructions

One Credit Only.—If property qualifies as more than one kind of energy property, you may take only one credit for the property.

Lines 1, 3, and 5—Type of Property.—For definition of recovery and nonrecovery

property, see the separate Instructions for Form 3468.

Line 1—Column (3).—Use the code letters from the following list to indicate the kind of property for which you are claiming a credit. If you enter more than one kind of property on a line, enter the code letter for each kind of property in column (3) and the code letter and dollar amount of each kind of property in the right hand margin.

The code letters are:

a. Alternative energy property, including biomass property

b. Specially defined energy property that reduces the energy consumed in an existing process, installed in connection with an existing industrial or commercial facility (see regulations section 1.48—9(f)).

c. Recycling equipment

d. Shale oil equipment

e. Equipment to produce natural gas from geopressured brine

f. Cogeneration equipment installed in an existing facility, but only if the cogeneration energy capacity of the facility is expanded. See section 48(l)(14).

g. Qualified intercity buses (see section 48(l)(16)(C) for the limitation on qualified investment for intercity buses based on the increase in operating seating capacity).

Line 3.—Figure your qualified investment in hydroelectric generating property. If the installed capacity is more than 25 megawatts, the 11% energy credit is allowed for only part of the qualified investment. See section 48(l)(13)(C).

In the space provided in line 3, enter the megawatts capacity of the generator as shown on the nameplate of the generator.

Line 5—Column (3).—Use the code letters from the following list to indicate the kind of property for which you are claiming a credit. Be sure to put the code or codes on the line for the correct recovery period or life years as explained in the instruction for line 1, column (3).

h. Solar equipment (but not passive solar equipment)

i. Wind equipment

j. Ocean thermal equipment

k. Geothermal equipment

See sections 48(l)(4) and 48(l)(3)(A)(viii) and (ix) for definitions and special rules that apply to these kinds of property.

STEP 7 (FORM 1040-ES)

Fred expects approximately the same income and tax situation for 1983, so he fills out Form 1040-ES's worksheet accordingly:

A. On Line 1 he enters the income he expects in 1983.
B. He enters this amount again on Line 3.
C. He enters his exemption on Line 4 and subtracts it from Line 3, entering the amount on Line 5.
D. He figures his tax on Line 6 using the Tax Rate Schedules; he enters this amount again on Lines 8 and 10.
E. On Line 12 he estimates his writing income and figures his estimated Social Security tax.
F. He totals Lines 10 and 12 on Line 14.
G. He estimates how much will be withheld from his meat-packing job and enters this on Line 15b and Line 16.
H. He subtracts Line 16 from Line 14 and enters the amount on Line 17. This is the estimated tax he should pay in 1983.
I. Fred divides this amount by four (4) and enters the amount on Line 18.
J. Fred fills out the first Payment Voucher and enters the amount he will pay during this quarter. (Unless his income increases or decreases, he will pay this amount again on June 15, September 15, and January 15 for 1984.) The reason Fred's estimated taxes are higher this year than last is due primarily to the fact that he does not have an investment credit to claim in 1983 as he did in 1982.

STEP 8 (GENERAL)

A. Fred staples (or clips) all of his forms and schedules together (except his Form 1040-ES worksheet, which he keeps).
B. On the front, he clips his employer's W-2 wage form and his check for $707 ($239 tax owed for 1982 plus $468 first installment of 1983 estimated taxes).

1983 Estimated Tax Worksheet (Keep for your records—Do Not Send to Internal Revenue Service)			
1 Enter amount of Adjusted Gross Income you expect in 1983		**1**	*$20,300* —
2 a If you plan to itemize deductions, enter the estimated total of your deductions. If you do not plan to itemize deductions, skip to line 2c and enter zero . .	**2a**		
b Enter { $3,400 if married filing a joint return (or qualifying widow(er)) . . } { $2,300 if single (or head of household) . . . . } { $1,700 if married filing a separate return . . . . }	**2b**		
c Subtract line 2b from line 2a (if zero or less, enter zero)		**2c**	0 —
d If you do not itemize deductions, enter your allowable deduction, if any, for charitable contributions (see page 13 of the 1982 Instructions for Form 1040)		**2d**	
3 Subtract line 2c or 2d, whichever applies, from line 1		**3**	*$20,300* —
4 Exemptions (multiply $1,000 times number of personal exemptions)		**4**	*$1,000* —
5 Subtract line 4 from line 3		**5**	*$19,300* —
6 Tax. (Figure your tax on line 5 by using Tax Rate Schedule X, Y, or Z in these instructions. DO NOT use the Tax Table or Tax Rate Schedule X, Y, or Z in the 1982 Form 1040 Instructions.)		**6**	*$3,535* —
7 Enter any additional taxes (see line 7 Instruction)		**7**	
8 Add lines 6 and 7		**8**	*$3,535* —
9 Credits (credit for the elderly, credit for child and dependent care expenses, investment credit, residential energy credit, etc.)		**9**	
10 Subtract line 9 from line 8		**10**	*$3,535* —
11 Tax from recapture of investment credit		**11**	
12 Estimate of 1983 self-employment income $ *5,300* ; if $35,700 or more, enter $3,337.95; if less, multiply the amount by .0935 (see line 12 Instruction for additional information)		**12**	*$496* —
13 Tax on premature distributions from an IRA		**13**	
14 Add lines 10 through 13		**14**	*$4,031* —
15 a Earned income credit	**15a**		
b Estimated income tax withheld and to be withheld (including income tax withholding on interest and dividends) during 1983	**15b** $2,800 —		
c Credit for Federal tax on special fuels and oils (see Form 4136)	**15c**		
16 Total (add lines 15a, b, and c)		**16**	*$2,800* —
17 Estimated tax (subtract line 16 from line 14). If $300 or more, fill out and file the payment-voucher along with your payment; if less, no payment is required at this time		**17**	*$1,169* —
Caution: You are required to prepay at least 80% of your tax liability each year. If you prepay less than 80% of your actual tax liability you will be subject to a penalty (see Instruction E). To avoid this, make sure your estimate is as accurate as possible. If you are unsure of your estimate, you may want to pay more than 80% of the amount you have estimated. In determining the amount of your estimated tax, you may take into account any of the four exceptions to the underpayment penalty. For more information on these exceptions, please get **Publication 505.**			
18 If the first payment you are required to make is due April 15, 1983, enter ¼ of line 17 here and on line 1 of your payment-voucher. You may round off cents to the nearest whole dollar. If you wish to pay more estimated tax than is shown on line 17, you may do so		**18**	*$468* —

Tear off here

- -

Form **1040-ES** | **1983**
Department of the Treasury Internal Revenue Service | Payment-Voucher

OMB No. 1545–0087

Return this voucher with check or money order payable to the Internal Revenue Service. Please do not send cash or staple your payment to this voucher. | (Calendar year—Due Jan. 17, 1984)

	Your social security number	Spouse's number, if joint payment
1 Amount of payment $ *468.00*	*000 - 00 - 0000*	
	First name and middle initial (of both spouses if joint payment)	Last name
2 Fiscal year filers enter year ending	*Fred E.*	*Lance*
	Address (Number and street)	
- - - - - - - - - - - - - - (month and year)	*2100 Maple St.*	
	City, State, and ZIP code	
	Maple City, IL 60000	

Please type or print

For Paperwork Reduction Act Notice, see instructions on page 1.

Appendix I

Figures for the Future

FUTURE SOCIAL SECURITY TAX FIGURES
(SELF-EMPLOYMENT PERCENTAGES)

1982–1984	9.35%
1985	9.90%
1986	10.00%

The minimum and maximum amounts taxable under Social Security change with the cost of living. As a result it is impossible to predict the future maximums and minimums. In 1983 the minimum income amount taxable is $400. The maximum income amount taxable is $35,700. (See Chapter 5 for further explanation.)

FUTURE ESTIMATED TAX FIGURES

You may have to file a Declaration of Estimated Tax if your estimated tax (over the amounts already withheld through wages paid by employer, etc.) is more than:

$300 in 1983
$400 in 1984
$500 in 1985

There are five exceptions the IRS allows for not paying estimated taxes even though you have not paid in the required 80% by the end of the year. However, these are very specific and very complex and in most cases would not apply to the average writer. If you wish to look into them, though, you can obtain IRS Publication 505, *Tax Withholding and Estimated Tax*.

FUTURE ACRS DEPRECIATION PERCENTAGES

Three-Year Property

Year	1981–1984	1985	1986
1	25%	29%	33%
2	38%	47%	45%
3	37%	24%	22%

Five-Year Property

1	15%	18%	20%
2	22%	33%	32%
3	21%	25%	24%
4	21%	16%	16%
5	21%	8%	8%

Ten-Year Property

1	8%	9%	10%
2	14%	19%	18%
3	12%	16%	16%
4	10%	14%	14%

5	10%	12%	12%
6	10%	10%	10%
7	9%	8%	8%
8	9%	6%	6%
9	9%	4%	4%
10	9%	2%	2%

FUTURE FIRST-YEAR EXPENSING (AMOUNTS)

1982–1983 $ 5,000 maximum ($2,500 married and filing separately)

1984–1985 $ 7,500 maximum ($3,750 married and filing separately)

1986 $10,000 maximum ($5,000 married and filing separately)

Appendix II

Additional Reading (IRS Pamphlets)

You have undoubtedly seen the phrase *see an accountant or other tax professional* in many sections of the book. The recommendation is made when certain tax laws (codes or regulations) become more complex than it makes sense to go into in this book or when there are so many different potential situations that it would be inappropriate to attempt to discuss them all.

As was pointed out in the book's introduction, if you are a "normal" writer with "normal" income sources and "normal" expenses, this book should really be all you need to figure your own taxes and claim maximum deductions. If you have some unique and/or complex situations that the book does not discuss, professional help is a viable alternative.

However, before you do contact an accountant or other tax professional to help you with these situations, you may wish to do a little further reading on your own. The best place to start is with the series of IRS pamphlets that you can obtain free from IRS offices (or can have mailed to you by calling your local IRS office toll-free). You can often find the answers to your additional questions in these.

Here is a list of the ones currently available that would be directly applicable to you as a freelance writer.

Publication Number	Title
—	*Instructions for preparing Form 1040 and instructions for Schedules A, B, C, D, E, F, R, RP, and SE*
17	*Your Federal Income Tax*
334	*Tax Guide for Small Business*
463	*Travel, Entertainment, and Gift Expenses*
505	*Tax Withholding and Estimated Tax*
508	*Educational Expenses*
533	*Self-Employment Tax*
534	*Depreciation*
535	*Business Expenses*
538	*Accounting Periods and Methods*
552	*Recordkeeping for Individuals and a List of Tax Publications* (lists other publications that might be of general tax interest)
560	*Tax Information on Self-Employed Retirement Plans*
572	*Investment Credit*
583	*Information for Business Taxpayers—Business Taxes, Identification Numbers, Recordkeeping*
587	*Business Use of Your Home*
590	*Tax Information on Individual Retirement Arrangements*

If you really become ambitious, you may wish to read the information "direct from the source": the Internal Revenue Code and/or the Internal Revenue Regulations (one or both of which may be available at your local library).

Appendix III
Worksheets
(for Reproduction)

WORKSHEET 1: ANNUAL INCOME

Year _____

Date	Received From	For	Amount

WORKSHEET 2: MONTHLY EXPENSES

Month _____ Year _____

Date	Payable To	Check #	Receipt Obtained	Expense Code*	Amount of Chk	Amount Attrib. to Bus.

*Expense Codes

1 Advertising
2 Bank Charges
3 Car and Truck Expenses
4 Dues and Publications
5 Education
6 Insurance
7 Interest
8 Legal and Professional Expenses
9 Office Supplies and Postage
10 Rent

11 Repairs
12 Taxes
13 Travel and Entertainment (and Gifts)
14 Utilities and Telephone
15 Wages
16 Photographs
17 Duplication
18 First-Year Expensing
19 Miscellaneous

WORKSHEET 3: STANDARD MILEAGE ALLOWANCE

Date	Description	Purpose	Mileage			(x) Rate	(=) Amount
			Start	End	Total		

WORKSHEET 4: ACTUAL OPERATING COSTS
(Itemized Auto Expenses)

Mileage at end of year _____

Mileage at beginning of year − _____

Total miles driven during year _____

Total business miles driven during year _____

Percent of vehicle use for business _____%
(total business miles ÷ total miles)

Individual expenses

auto club membership $_____

bridge/road tolls $_____

depreciation of vehicle $_____

depreciation on misc. items $_____

fluids/lubricants/etc. $_____

garage rent $_____

gasoline $_____

insurance $_____

interest $_____

licenses/plates/stickers/etc. $_____

misc. deductible items $_____

parking costs $_____

repairs $_____

state and local taxes $_____

towing $_____

washing and waxing + $_____

Total individual expenses $_____

Percentage of business use (from above) _____%

Total deductible $_____

WORKSHEET 5: COMPARISON OF ITEMIZED AUTO EXPENSES VERSUS STANDARD MILEAGE ALLOWANCE

Standard Mileage Allowance

Total amount (from business miles driven) (Total of Worksheet 3)	$_____
Interest (on purchase of vehicle)	$_____
State/local taxes (on purchase of vehicle)	$_____
Parking fees and bridge/road tolls	+ $_____
Total amount deductible	$_____

Itemized Auto Expenses (Actual Operating Costs)

Total from Worksheet 4 $_____

Which is larger?

☐ Standard Mileage Allowance

☐ Actual Operating Costs

Choose this method for the year.*

_____

* See Chapter 7 for limitations on choice based on use of depreciation.

WORKSHEET 6: HOME OFFICE

Total area of home (square feet) _____

Total area of home office (square feet) _____

Percentage of area for home office _____%
    (area of home office ÷ total area)

First Classification Expenses

Item	Total	(×)	%	(=)	Amt.
Mortgage Interest	$_____		____%		$_____
Real Estate Taxes	$_____		____%		+ $_____
Total					$_____

Second Classification Expenses

Item	Total	(×)	%	(=)	Amt.
Rent	$_____		____%		$_____
Utilities					
Gas/Oil	$_____		____%		$_____
Electricity	$_____		____%		$_____
Water	$_____		____%		$_____
Trash Removal	$_____		____%		$_____
Insurance	$_____		____%		$_____
Repairs	$_____		____%		$_____
Misc. (maid service, cleaning, etc.)	$_____		____%		$_____
Total					$_____

Third Classification Expenses

Item	Depreciable Amount
Depreciation on Office Itself (from Worksheet 7)	$_____
Depreciation on Improvements (based on percentage of value to home office; see Chapter 7)	$_____
Total	$_____
Total (all three classifications)	$_____

WORKSHEET 7: DEPRECIABLE ASSETS

Item										
Placed in Service										
Type of Depreciation										
Value										
Life										
Year	%	$	%	$	%	$	%	$	%	$
1981										
1982										
1983										
1984										
1985										
1986										
1987										
1988										
1989										
1990										
1991										
1992										
1993										
1994										
1995										
1996										
1997										
1998										
1999										
2000										
Total										

Index

Boldface numbers indicate the pages on which the topics are defined and explained most thoroughly.